THE BIG BOOK OF USELESS KNOWLEDGE

250 OF THE Coolest, Weirdest, AND MOST Unbelievable Facts

YOU WON'T BE TAUGHT IN SCHOOL

NEON  SQUID

CONTENTS

Dr. Brittney G. Borowiec is a scientist and science writer based in Canada. She studies how fish cope with environmental challenges like being too hot or not having enough oxygen to breathe. Outside of the lab, she writes about weird animals doing amazing things and dotes on her very large and very fluffy cat, Ranger.

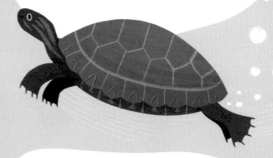

Laura Buller is an editor and writer. There are countless things Laura did not learn in school. That is why she loves working on children's books—because you never stop learning.

Dr. Victoria Atkinson started her scientific career at the age of five, making a mess across the kitchen floor with baking soda volcano experiments and growing colorful crystals all over the window ledge! More than 20 years later, she graduated from the University of Oxford and now works as a science writer, specialising in chemistry.

ABOUT THE AUTHORS & ILLUSTRATORS

Anna Goldfield is a podcaster, science writer, illustrator, archaeologist, and creator of all sorts of content to introduce people to the study of the world around us and its past. Anna works on the kids' science podcast *Brains On!* and presents the archaeology podcast *The Dirt*.

Sophie Allan is Head of Teaching and Learning for the UK National Space Academy. She lectures on space engineering and creates programmes on space education for the European Space Agency, UK Space Agency, and more. Her work has reached over 4 million people to date!

Hannah Li is an award-winning Chinese illustrator based in New York, USA. Her artistic odyssey began with childhood doodles, evolving into captivating illustrations known for their optimism, soothing qualities, and emotional depth. When she's not drawing, she's on a quest for spicy food, which fuels her creative fire.

Dr. Lucia Perez Diaz is an Earth scientist and author-illustrator from the magical land of Galicia in northern Spain. She investigates what our planet looked like through geological time—a detective of sorts, trying to build a time machine from spare parts scattered across our planet's surface. She loves writing about science because, like all good nerds, she enjoys telling people about what she does, why it is cool, and why they should learn all about it!

Alexander Mostov is a Seattle-based illustrator who makes playful, inclusive illustrations for everything from picture books to apps. His books include *The Secret Life of Spies* and *Nikola Tesla: Little People, Big Dreams*. When not drawing, Alexander can be found munching on bread or riding his little silver motorcycle through the countryside.

Dr. Yara Haridy is a paleontologist and science communicator who looks at how our skeletons evolved over eons. Yara's affinity for the natural world took root during her upbringing in the Middle East, where she cultivated a fascination for collecting snails and nurturing birds.

Liz Kay is an illustrator based in West Yorkshire, UK. She loves all things illustration and having adventures with her little family. Liz's books include *The History of Everywhere* and *My Met Sticker Collection*.

CHAPTER 1

USELESS NATURE KNOWLEDGE

In which the reader will encounter wombats that poo cubes,
crab imposters, dolphin spies, beetles that like stargazing,
toxic trees, and meat-eating plants.

SQUIRT!

INFLATE!

FREEZE!

RUN!

Nobody wants to be someone else's dinner, but horned lizards take it to the extreme. If a predator comes sniffing around, they freeze, hoping they go unnoticed, and sprint off if the opportunity presents itself. Cornered horned lizards, however, have to get creative. And what better way to put off a predator than to squirt blood FROM THEIR EYES. They do this by bursting blood vessels around their eyes. They also puff up like a spiky balloon so they can't be swallowed. These lizards don't go down without fight!

BLACK
ON WHITE, OR
WHITE
ON BLACK?

Nice coat, bro.

If you ever decided you wanted to shave a zebra, you would find that their skin is black, even under their white stripes. The reason for zebras' fashionable coats is still a mystery, but scientists think that the stripes may dazzle and confuse flies. In fact, cows and horses who have been painted like zebras don't get bitten by bugs as often. Not all striped animals are the same underneath—tigers have striped skin! Polar bears, meanwhile, have long white fur and black skin.

MONKEYS WASH USING
THEIR OWN PEE

There's no soap or hand sanitizer in the animal kingdom, so tufted capuchin monkeys turn to the next best thing: they wash their hands and feet with their pee. At first, scientists thought they peed on themselves to cool down or to mark their territory, but that doesn't seem to be the case. Now they think that monkeys might pee-wash to attract mates with the smell, to ward off fights with other monkeys, or just to help them relax!

WOMBATS POOP CUBES

You may be interested to find out that wombat poop is cuboid—it's stackable like building blocks! The cube shape comes from their unusual intestine, which has just the right combination of stiff and flexible sections to form the poop into blocks as it moves through their body. No one knows why wombats poop cubes. One idea is that the cube shape helps wombats mark their territory. Cubes don't roll away like rounder shapes, so wombats can confidently leave piles of poop on uneven surfaces like rocks and logs.

Won't be a second!

LET'S GET TO THE BOTTOM OF THIS

Many turtles spend the winter buried deep in the mud at the bottom of ponds. But how do they breathe through all that gunk, water, and ice? Well, through their butts of course! The turtle's butthole (called a cloaca) is lined with blood vessels that take oxygen out of the water, so the turtle doesn't have to breathe with its mouth and nose. Some turtles also use the oxygen they get from their rear ends to dive underwater for longer when looking for food.

MEET A VERY STINKY CABBAGE

Cabbage isn't exactly known for smelling good when cooked, but the eastern skunk cabbage takes smelling bad to a whole new level! This North American plant warms itself up when it blooms in late winter, getting hot enough to melt the snow around it. The warm air also makes a tiny breeze as it moves through the cabbage's leaves, spreading its stench everywhere to attract insects to pollinate it.

And I thought I was bad...

SECRETS OF THE SLOTHS

Sloths live a slow, quiet life. But delve beneath the surface and all is not as it seems... These mammals grow algae in their fur! The sloths are quite happy about this, as the algae provides camouflage in the forest, as well as extra snacks. But the algae doesn't just grow on its own: the sloths farm it with the help of sloth moths! These moths lay their eggs in sloth poop, and as adults they live in the sloth's fur, where they fertilize the algae. A sloth carries a whole ecosystem in its fur!

SUPERSTRONG

Some bugs are unsquishable! The diabolical ironclad beetle is so strong that it can be run over by a car and walk away totally fine. The beetle's outer shell, called an exoskeleton, gets its strength from two features: thick layers of protein and interlocking zipper-like joints, both of which help it to spread out and absorb crushing forces. Engineers are trying to copy the beetle's exoskeleton to make sturdier airplanes, bridges, and buildings.

HEY, ARE YOU REALLY A CRAB?

"I'm going to pretend you didn't say that."

Hermit crab

"I'M DEFINITELY A CRAB!"

King crab

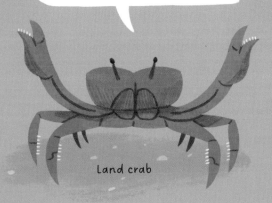

"Of course I'm a crab, look at me!"

Land crab

What do king crabs, porcelain crabs, hairy stone crabs, hermit crabs, and horseshoe crabs have in common? They are not real crabs! These imposters have a crab-like shape but are not closely related to true crabs (the infraorder Brachyura). You can tell a true crab apart from a fake crab by its legs: true crabs have four pairs of long legs but fake crabs only have three (plus one pair of short legs).

"I COME FROM A LONG LINE OF CRABS... MY MOTHER WAS A CRAB, MY FATHER WAS A CRAB. MY UNCLE PAUL WAS A CRAB."

"Ask me that again and I'll pincer you."

Hermit crab

Coconut crab

You'd think getting swallowed by a frog would be the end of the line for a bug. Not if you're a beetle with a tough shell and a lot of determination! Some beetles can survive being swallowed, and then it's time to plot their escape. There are two directions in which they can go. Japanese water beetles head south, crawling through the frog's guts before walking out its butt. Bombardier beetles are even worse—they spray a nasty chemical that makes the frog vomit them back up!

Was that a fart?

SOMETIMES DINNER CRAWLS BACK OUT...

12

WOODPECKER
TONGUE-TWISTER

Woodpeckers hammer holes in trees and scoop out tasty grubs with their long, sticky tongues. But where does a woodpecker store its superlong tongue after it's done eating? It wraps it around its brain! The tongue splits into a Y-shape in the woodpecker's throat, before looping around the back of their head. Sometimes the tongue is so long the tip ends up in the back of the bird's nostril!

UNDERWATER SPIES

The future of warfare is interesting. Who do you want on your side? Soldiers? Aritificial intelligence? How about dolphins and sea lions? Believe it or not, the United States Navy Marine Mammal Program trains these underwater mammals to conduct military missions. The animals learn how to guard harbors, find mines underwater, and retrieve lost equipment with their supercharged underwater senses. Dolphins' natural sonar (they can locate objects using echoes) and sea lions' excellent low-light vision and agility outperform human divers and robots. As of 2019, there were about 70 dolphins and 30 sea lions working as spies in the programme, which is based in San Diego, California.

THE **SMALLEST DOG** IN THE WORLD IS **THE CHIHUAHUA.** YOU MAY HAVE SEEN THEM BEING CARRIED AROUND IN HANDBAGS!

SMALL **DOG** SYNDROME

Dogs mark their territory by peeing on trees, lampposts, and other tall objects. That is also why dogs like to sniff these things—they want to learn who else is around. But dogs also lie, especially the little ones. Small dogs tilt their legs up and "shoot high" when they mark their territory with pee, tricking other dogs into thinking they are taller and scarier than they really are!

DOGS EVOLVED FROM **WOLVES** ABOUT 20,000 YEARS AGO.

THE BEETLE
ASTRONOMER

What do ancient sailors and dung beetles have in common? They use the stars to find their way home! Dung beetles sniff out mounds of poop left by other animals and roll them into a large ball they can snack on later. To find their way back to base, the beetles stand up on their poop balls and observe the night sky. They take a mental snapshot of the Milky Way, the galaxy that our solar system is in, and use it as a map to find their way. Clever, huh?

MOSQUITOES LOVE THE SMELL OF STINKY CHEESE

What do humans smell like to other animals? I'm afraid to say that the answer is cheese. Mosquitoes love the musty smell of bacteria like *Brevibacterium epidermidis* that live on the rind of soft, smelly cheeses. The same bacteria lives between our toes and under our nails, making feet and dirty socks stinky. Mosquitoes love the smell of stinky feet so much that we might be able to use smelly cheese as bait to distract them from biting people.

HORSESHOE CRAB BLOOD COSTS $60,000 PER GALLON

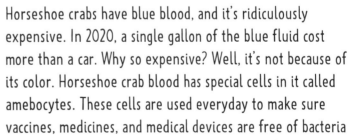

Horseshoe crabs have blue blood, and it's ridiculously expensive. In 2020, a single gallon of the blue fluid cost more than a car. Why so expensive? Well, it's not because of its color. Horseshoe crab blood has special cells in it called amebocytes. These cells are used everyday to make sure vaccines, medicines, and medical devices are free of bacteria and safe for use in people. This is great for people, but not good for the crabs, who are farmed for their blood in large numbers.

THE ANIMAL THAT SMELLS LIKE POPCORN

The forests of Southeast Asia smell like wood, rain, and... popcorn? That's the smell of a shaggy ferret-like creature called a binturong. Binturongs spend their time wandering through treetops, looking for fruits, birds, insects, and other snacks. The popcorn smell comes from a chemical in their pee. Male binturongs are extra stinky and might attract mates or mark their territory with their stench.

THE 32,000-YEAR-OLD SEEDS

A group of Russian scientists found ancient seeds in old squirrel burrows and decided they'd try to bring them back to life. They cloned the 32,000-year-old seeds in the lab, and from those clones grew flowers! The seeds were so well-preserved for two reasons: they were full of sugar, which stopped them from freezing, and they were underground, which protected them from the Sun's UV rays. The same species of flower is still around today, and has shorter petals than its ancestors.

DANGER!
WATCH OUT FOR THAT TREE

Remember when Snow White bit into the poisoned apple and fell into a deep sleep? She got off easy! Biting into the fruit of the manchineel tree causes burns, blisters, swelling, and will probably make you throw up. Every part of the tree is toxic, and its sap can even strip paint off cars. Despite all the dangers, people living in the American tropics sometimes use manchineel wood to make furniture, which is safe as long as the sap is dried.

DANGER

NO ENTRY

KEEP OUT

MALE PEACOCK
SPIDERS DANCE
LIKE THEIR **LIVES
DEPEND ON IT.**
THAT'S BECAUSE
THEY DO!

NUMEROUS BIRD
SPECIES LIKE TO DANCE,
FROM **FLAMINGOS** TO
SWANS, BUT **BIRDS OF
PARADISE** HAVE THE
BEST MOVES.

BOOGIE WITH THE ANIMALS

Think humans are the only animals who like to make an impression on the dancefloor? Think again. Male peacock spiders put on an elaborate show to woo potential mates. First, they fan out their colorful abdomens to get attention, just like a regular peacock. Then they vibrate to make spider music, sway, and clap their front legs together, doing their best to look handsome. The stakes are high! If the female spider is unimpressed, not only does the bachelor lose his chance to have babies, he might be gobbled up as a snack.

HONEY BEES DO SOMETHING CALLED A **WAGGLE DANCE** INSIDE THE HIVE TO LET OTHER BEES KNOW WHERE TO FIND THE **BEST FLOWERS**.

BLUE-FOOTED BOOBIES, ASIDE FROM HAVING A HILARIOUS NAME, LIKE TO STRUT THEIR STUFF. FEMALES ARE ATTRACTED TO THE BLUE FEET OF THE MALES, SO THE BOYS JIG THEM **UP AND DOWN** TO IMPRESS THEM!

WHALE EAR WAX RECORDS HISTORY

Whale ears slowly plug up with wax as they age. But instead of making it harder for them to hear, it actually makes it easier, by transferring soundwaves deeper into their ears. That's not the only cool thing about whale wax. Scientists can count the number of layers a wax plug has to estimate how old a whale is (like tree rings), and can even tell if the whale swam in polluted waters at some point in its life. Studying whale ear wax can tell scientists a lot about a whale's life!

THE EAR WAX GROWS IN LAYERS—ONE RING FOR EVERY YEAR!

OCTOPUSES HAVE NINE BRAINS

Think you're pretty smart? If you've only got one brain you'd better pipe down. An octopus has a small brain in each of its eight arms, and one big, doughnut-shaped brain in its head. That's nine in total! Octopuses and their relatives, such as squid, have a ton of brain power—their brains are the biggest of all invertebrates (animals without a backbone). Octopuses living in aquariums often escape, can solve puzzles and mazes, and will occasionally sneak out to snack on crabs and fish living in other tanks.

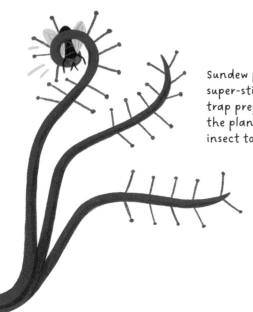

Sundew plants have super-sticky hairs that trap prey. Once caught, the plants curl around the insect to digest them.

Pinguicula conzattii's leaves are sticky like flypaper!

Philippine pitcher plants use sweet nectar to tempt bugs into their pool of doom.

Flies that investigate yellow pitcher plants often end up drowning.

Venus flytraps... trap flies.

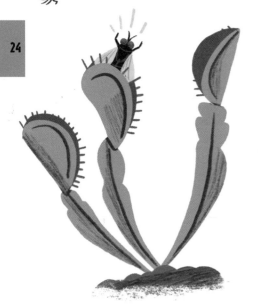

THERE ARE HUNDREDS OF MEAT-EATING PLANTS

Plants make food from air and sunlight. But some plants, actually a lot of plants, have more... savoury tastes. Nearly 600 species of plants are carnivores, meaning they eat animals such as insects! They snare animals with pools of acid, sticky mucus, or traps that snap shut. Most carnivorous plants live in poor quality soil like bogs, which is possible because of the extra nutrients they get from their high-protein diets.

THE FISH THAT CHANGE SEX

The same clown fish can be a male, a female, or neither at different parts of its life. All clown fish are born as neither males nor females, and develop into males as they age. The biggest male clown fish becomes a female, and the second biggest male clown fish becomes her mate. If the female dies or leaves, her partner becomes the new female leader, and the next fish in line becomes the new male leader. The clown fish mating system is called "sequential hermaphroditism."

CHAPTER 2

USELESS HUMAN BODY KNOWLEDGE

In which the reader will witness a sneeze racing a cheetah, discover how ancient Egyptian pregnancy tests worked, investigate why bald men used to rub onions on their heads, and find out why your brain likes to eat itself!

HUMANS PRODUCE ENOUGH SALIVA IN A LIFETIME TO FILL TWO SWIMMING POOLS

That's about a quarter of a gallon every day! It may be gross, but saliva is really important for keeping your mouth working properly—can you imagine trying to talk or eat with a completely dry mouth? Your disgusting dribble is mostly water but it also contains a mixture of enzymes—special substances that help to break down food in your mouth—and several chemicals that can kill bacteria trying to sneak into your body!

YOUR STOMACH
BLUSHES
WHEN YOU DO

We all blush when we feel embarrassed, but if you thought it was just your cheeks that blushed, think again! Embarrassment triggers our fight-or-flight response—one of our body's automatic reactions to danger. Now obviously there's nothing dangerous about feeling embarrassed, but your body reacts anyway, releasing a chemical called adrenaline into the blood. As adrenaline flows through you, it makes your blood vessels get wider, so they can deliver more oxygen to your muscles and help you escape the threat. Blood suddenly rushes to the surface of your skin, making you appear red-faced. If you could look in your stomach, the exact same thing would be happening!

THIS IS SO AWKWARD...

WHY DO I SOUND SO WEIRD?

Have you ever noticed that your voice sounds a bit weird on recordings? That's because to you at least, it is different! When you talk, the sound bounces around inside your mouth, head, and ears, creating thousands of tiny vibrations without you realizing. But other people can't sense those vibrations, so they hear your voice differently from how you do! When you listen to yourself in a recording, you're actually hearing yourself as other people do—without the vibrations. This means that while you sound the same to everyone else, to yourself your voice sounds weird and unfamiliar!

CAN YOU WIGGLE YOUR EARS?

PATHETIC...

Thousands of years ago humans could actually move their ears a bit like a cat. This was an important adaptation when people lived outside, and it helped them to hunt for food and avoid predators. Today, we don't need to worry about survival in the same way, so over time we lost the ability to move our ears. However, we're still born with the muscles that used to control them, so with lots of practice it's possible to learn how to wiggle your ears!

TICKLE TORTURE

It may seem harmless, but tickling people as a punishment has been used for centuries. The ancient Romans had a particularly strange method—they bathed criminals' feet in salt water and then left them to be licked by goats! The tickly sensation quickly went from funny to painful. When we're tickled our first instinct is to laugh, but if you've ever had a fit of the giggles you'll know that laughing for too long can actually start to make your stomach hurt. Roman prisoners were often tickled by goats for hours, so they probably felt very sore by the end!

IT'S NOT JUST HUMANS THAT LAUGH WHEN THEY'RE TICKLED. OUR APE COUSINS, INCLUDING **CHIMPANZEES** AND **GORILLAS**, DO TOO!

YOU CAN'T TICKLE YOURSELF BECAUSE TICKLING INVOLVES AN **ELEMENT OF SURPRISE** AND YOUR BRAIN KNOWS WHAT YOU'RE GOING TO DO!

YOU ARE GOLDEN!

Did you know there is gold inside you? About 0.007 ounces (200 milligrams) to be exact. But even this tiny amount makes a big impact! Gold is an excellent conductor of electricity and is often used in electronic devices like smartphones and speakers. The brain uses electronic signals to send messages around the body, so a little bit of gold is really useful! Scientists have also discovered that small amounts of gold help to keep joints healthy, but we still don't really understand why this is.

R.I.P. SKIN

The top 20 or so layers of your skin are dead. But no need to mourn, this is actually a good thing! The skin is the biggest organ of the human body and has two really important jobs—it helps protect you from infection and it makes sure your body doesn't lose too much water. All those dead layers are a really important barrier, preventing nasties from getting in and water from getting out! Your body makes around 40,000 new skin cells every day, so these layers are constantly recycled and you have a completely new skin every month or so.

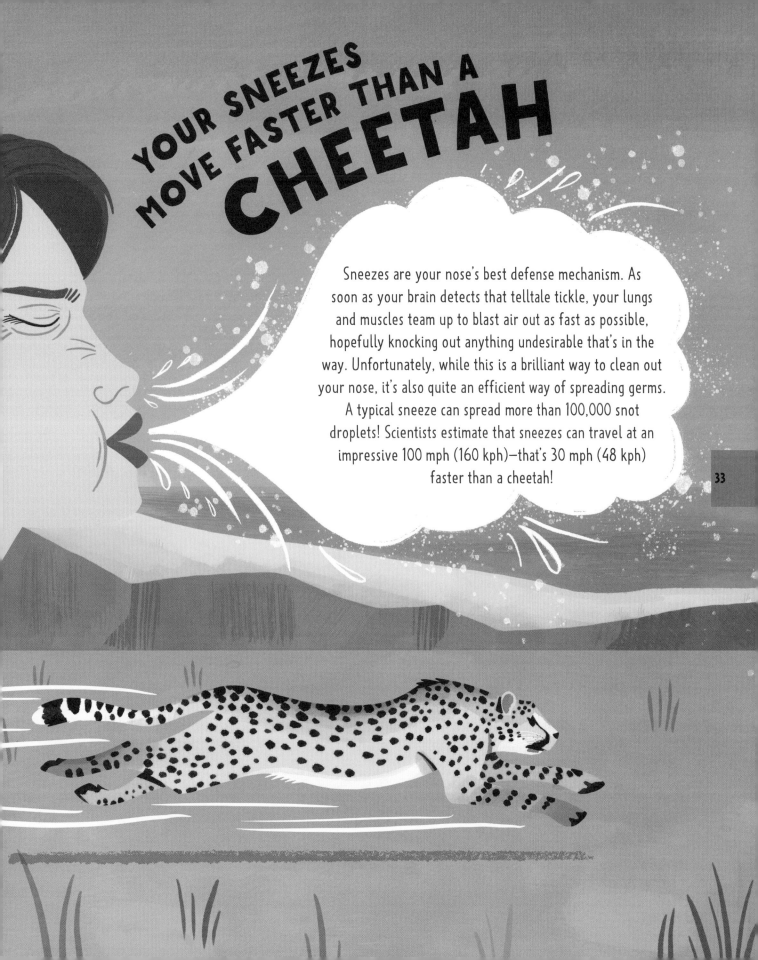

YOUR SNEEZES MOVE FASTER THAN A CHEETAH

Sneezes are your nose's best defense mechanism. As soon as your brain detects that telltale tickle, your lungs and muscles team up to blast air out as fast as possible, hopefully knocking out anything undesirable that's in the way. Unfortunately, while this is a brilliant way to clean out your nose, it's also quite an efficient way of spreading germs. A typical sneeze can spread more than 100,000 snot droplets! Scientists estimate that sneezes can travel at an impressive 100 mph (160 kph)—that's 30 mph (48 kph) faster than a cheetah!

Have you ever stayed in a bath too long and noticed that your fingers and toes have gone really wrinkly? It feels a bit weird and disgusting, but it's actually a really important adaptation! The pattern of wrinkles helps water drain away from your fingertips, making it easier to pick up and hold wet objects, which would otherwise be really slippy! Because we don't need this extra grip when our hands are dry, our bodies have evolved to only wrinkle when our hands are wet. Clever, huh?

POLAR BEARS HAVE LITTLE BUMPS ON THE SOLES OF THEIR PAWS THAT HELP THEM TO AVOID **SLIPPING ON ICE.**

IN PRAISE OF WRINKLY FINGERS

HUMANS AREN'T THE ONLY ANIMALS TO GET PRUNEY FINGERS. **MACAQUES** (A TYPE OF MONKEY) GET THEM TOO!

GECKOS GRIP TO WALLS THANKS TO **MICROSCOPIC HAIRS** ON THEIR FEET.

CHUCK HIM
IN A BOX OF
SOIL!

Have you soiled
yourself again, Jim?

The first sailors had very unhealthy diets.
Fruit and vegetables wouldn't keep on board
ships, so often the crew would go months and
months without eating any vitamins. During
long journeys, sailors would begin to develop
the terrible symptoms of a disease called
scurvy—bleeding, aching, and sometimes
even dying. Because this dreadful disease
only seemed to affect people at sea,
everyone assumed scurvy was caused by
being away from dry land, so ship captains
often carried huge boxes of soil. They hoped
that if they buried their ill crew members, it
might cure the disease!

YOUR FINGERNAILS GROW ABOUT THREE TIMES AS FAST AS YOUR TOENAILS

Which is definitely better than the other way around! Scientists think this could be because we use our hands more than our feet. Your body assumes your fingernails are being worn down more quickly than your toenails, so it needs to replace them more often. Your nails also grow faster on the hand you use most often, so if you're right-handed, the fingernails on your right hand will grow more quickly than on your left. Check it out next time you cut your nails!

I SPHINX YOU'RE PREGNANT

You can keep the wheat if you like?

The ancient Egyptians had pregnancy tests, and they worked in a very similar way to the ones today! When someone is pregnant their body starts producing a chemical called hCG, and pregnancy tests work by detecting this chemical in their urine. The ancient Egyptians knew that something in women's urine changed if they were pregnant, so hopeful mothers would pee into bags filled with barley or wheat. If the seeds started growing, that meant the woman was pregnant. We now know this is because hCG helps seeds germinate! This test was about 70 percent accurate, which isn't bad for 4,000-year-old technology!

THE ACID IN YOUR STOMACH IS STRONG ENOUGH TO DISSOLVE METAL

JUST TO BE CLEAR—DO NOT EVER EAT METAL!

Your stomach is full of a mixture of chemicals called gastric juice, which help to break down food. One of the most important of these chemicals is hydrochloric acid. Scientists measure the strength of acids using something called the pH scale, and the stuff in your stomach scores about 1.5. But this doesn't mean it's a weak acid—in fact, the lower the score, the stronger the acid—so your gastric juice is powerful enough to dissolve steel! At this point you might be wondering why this acid doesn't start dissolving a hole in you... Luckily the stomach protects itself by secreting layers of mucus!

Everyone knows someone who claims to be double-jointed. But the truth is that everybody has the same number of joints—it just happens that some people can move theirs much farther than usual, and even contort themselves into strange shapes. Inside your joints are an important group of stringy materials called ligaments and tendons. Ligaments act like ropes and hold the bones together, and tendons join the muscles on to the bones. Very flexible people are often called double-jointed but really they just have stretchier ligaments and tendons!

THERE'S NO SUCH THING AS BEING DOUBLE-JOINTED

YOU'VE GOT THE GUTS FOR THIS GAME

Intestines are fleshy tubes responsible for absorbing nutrients from the food digested in your stomach. To do this properly they need a huge surface area. The average adult has about 26 ft (8 m) of intestine—it may sound like a lot but, spread out, this would only cover about four pieces of A4 paper! Fortunately, our intestines are covered in lots of fingerlike tendrils called villi, which increase the surface area more than 100 times. So with the villi, our intestines would actually cover half a badminton court, or more than 600 pieces of letter-size paper!

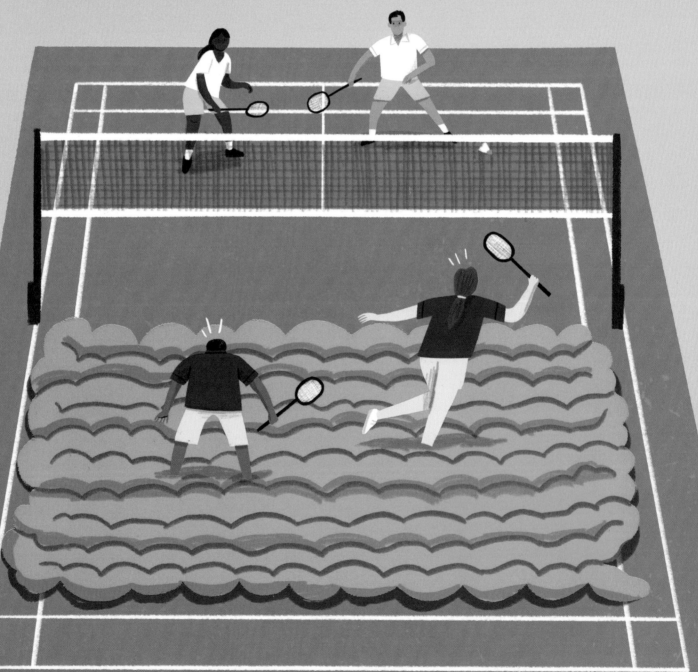

FED UP OF BEING BALD?

TRY RUBBING AN ONION ON YOUR HEAD!

In the 1800s bald men rubbed onions on their heads. A crazy idea, right? But people used to believe that this would make their hair grow back! Although onions have never been scientifically investigated as a cure for baldness, some of the chemistry at work inside this pungent vegetable could be good for the body. Several of the substances in onions have antibacterial properties that can help protect the scalp from infections, while other chemicals called antioxidants may protect the hair from other types of damage. Surprisingly, you can still buy onion juice as a hair product—there's just no guarantee that it will work!

A NOSE AHEAD
AT THE FINISHING LINE!

When running a long distance, the way that you breathe is much more important than how you move your legs. To keep all of their muscles going for such a long time, marathon runners need to maximize the amount of oxygen they take in with each breath, and symmetrical nostrils help them breathe more efficiently! The opposite is true for sprint runners—in short races, good breathing doesn't matter as much and it's how you move your legs that's important. So people with symmetrical knees actually make better sprinters.

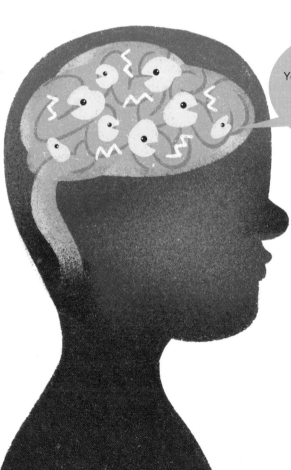

You've got to try the frontal lobe.

YOUR BRAIN IS CONSTANTLY EATING ITSELF

But never fear, this is a good thing! The brain takes charge of everything happening in the body, but unfortunately, all of the chemical reactions involved in this complicated business produce quite a lot of trash. Special cells called phagocytes are responsible for keeping the brain tidy and eat up all of these waste chemicals. However, they also have an unexpected second job—eating your actual brain cells! Surprisingly, eating itself helps the brain to stay healthy by getting rid of old cells and making it easier to form new brain connections. Genius!

FOOD TASTES DIFFERENT ON PLANES

People often complain that the food on airplanes is disgusting, but it turns out this isn't actually the chef's fault! Once up in the air, the lower pressure and drier air really affect our taste buds, and it becomes much harder for us to detect sweet and salty flavors. Unfortunately, bitter and sour tastes don't really change, so it's surprisingly difficult to make something that doesn't taste horrible!

YOU'RE TALLER FIRST THING IN THE MORNING

Yes, you! Although probably by less than an inch. Your spine is made up of 33 separate pieces of bone called vertebrae, each separated by a piece of softer material called cartilage. When you lie down at night, all of these separate pieces of your spine spread out a little. This means that when you get up in the morning, your backbone will be a bit longer than when you went to bed. During the day, the effects of gravity gradually compress the pieces of bone and cartilage closer together, so by the time you go back to bed again you've shrunk back to normal!

THE AVERAGE PERSON SPENDS MORE THAN 300 DAYS ON THE TOILET DURING THEIR LIFETIME

Won't be a minute!

Which sounds like a lot, but spread over about 80 years isn't so bad! Most people tend to go to the toilet between four and ten times a day, probably spending around 15 minutes on the throne in total. Multiply that by 365 and, over a year, that's 5,475 minutes (or around 91 hours) using the can! So during an 80-year life, a person will spend a whopping 7,300 hours, or more than 300 days, on the toilet! No wonder some people take a good book to read...

ITCH OR OUCH?

Nerve cells deliver messages to your brain from all around the body, but some of these messages travel faster than others. If something is causing pain, we need to be able to react quickly and protect the body, so these messages rush toward the brain at an impressive 80 mph (130 kph). But less important information, like telling your brain that you've got an itchy arm, doesn't need as quick a response, so these messages snail their way along the nerve cells at just 2 mph (3 kph)—that's 40 times slower!

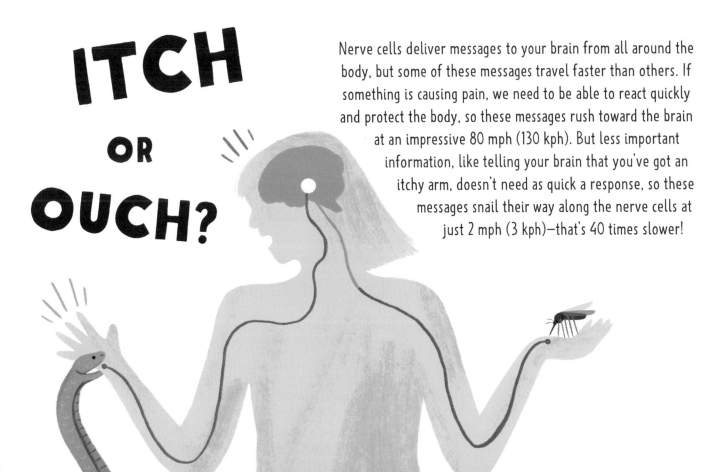

Reflexes are one of our body's best defense mechanisms—lightning fast reactions that enable us to respond quickly to dangers around us. But measurements taken over the last 150 years show that our reflexes are actually getting slower, not faster. This puzzled scientists at first—people now are much healthier than 150 years ago, so surely we'd expect to be quicker? However, since the 1880s we've also been getting consistently taller. Taller people have longer nerve cells, so messages from the brain take longer to travel because they've got farther to go!

Owww! I wish I was a baby.

BABY KNEECAPS AREN'T MADE OF BONE

Babies still have kneecaps, but they're made of a softer material called cartilage. Learning to walk is a tricky process and toddlers fall over lots of times before they get the hang of it. But because cartilage is a bit more bendy than bone, it doesn't hurt so much when they hit the floor! Kneecaps start to harden after about the age of two (when most children have already learnt to walk) and usually become fully bone by the age of ten.

CARTILAGE IS THE SAME STUFF YOUR EARS AND NOSE ARE MADE OF.

You're certainly crying like one!

OSTRICHES HAVE A **DOUBLE KNEECAP** (THAT'S TWO PER LEG) AND NO ONE KNOWS WHY.

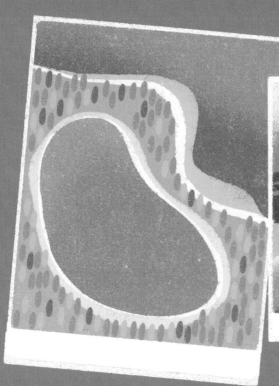

CHAPTER 3

USELESS PLACES KNOWLEDGE

In which the reader will learn what's hidden behind the giant heads of Mount Rushmore, voyage to an island inhabited by deadly snakes, discover why the Eiffel Tower in Paris is growing, and find out what item of food was used to build the Great Wall of China.

MEGACITY CROSSING

The United Nations defines a megacity as one with a population of 10 million people or more. There are more than 30 megacities in the world, with Tokyo, Japan, topping the list. Some 37,274,000 people crowd the city. Every time the light turns green at Shibuya Crossing in the city center, around 2,500 people cross the street!

THE ECHO SOUNDS LIKE A BIRD CALLED A **RESPLENDENT QUETZAL.**

DO YOU HEAR BIRDS?

You have to applaud the amazing Maya people who built the pyramid of Chichén Itzá in Mexico. But if you clap your hands at the base of this structure, something strange happens. You'll hear an echo that sounds like the chirp of a bird that was considered sacred by the Maya! Get a round of applause going, and you'll hear a chorus of chirps that seem to roll down the side of the pyramid.

THE FORBIDDEN ISLAND

Forget about a holiday to India's North Sentinel Island. It's against Indian law to visit there, and the 150 or so Sentinelese residents will defend their privacy in any way they can. Visitors tend to be killed, although the Sentinelese have accepted gifts of coconuts. The islanders are one of the few uncontacted groups left in the world. Their ancestors have lived on the island for 60,000 years.

The giant heads of Mount Rushmore in South Dakota, USA, are hiding a secret... Tucked behind Abraham Lincoln is a special chamber. Inside the chamber is a vault. Inside the vault is a box. The sculptor of Mount Rushmore, Gutzon Borglum, hoped famous American documents like the Constitution could be housed there, guarded by an enormous and cool bronze eagle. After his death, the plans were scaled down. Instead the box contains plates engraved with the story of the monument and a short history of the US. Perhaps the 21 ft (6.4 m) long noses and nostrils would have been better storage places?

WHAT'S INSIDE YOUR HEAD?

DO NOT ENTER!

The Lascaux caves in France were discovered in 1940, when four teenagers walking their dog lost it down a hole. When they climbed down to rescue the pup, they discovered one of the world's finest examples of prehistoric art on the cave walls. Tourists swarmed to the site, but their breath and sweat made it damp, stinky, and posed a danger to the fragile paintings. Today, you can only visit a replica.

THE ART IN THE LASCAUX CAVES IS ESTIMATED TO BE **17,000 YEARS OLD!**

WHEN IN ROME

When Rome's incredible Colosseum opened in 80 CE, Emperor Titus celebrated with 100 days of games, exotic animal shows, prisoner executions, and gladiator fights. Some 50,000 Romans packed the arena to enjoy the free spectacles and munch on free food (archaeologists are still digging up discarded nutshells and seeds today). But you had to have a ticket! Numbers scratched onto broken bits of pottery directed people to their aisles. Spectators had to be careful about eating too many snacks, though—the smallest seats were only 14 in (35 cm) wide!

BEWARE OF
SNAKES

Ilha de Queimada Grande off the coast of Brazil is also known as Snake Island. Here you will find (although it is best not to find) venomous golden lancehead pit vipers. These dangerous reptiles got stuck on the island when rising sea levels during the last ice age separated them from the mainland. Only a few scientists and navy crews are allowed to visit the island, even though the snakes prefer to eat birds.

THE EIFFEL TOWER IS GROWING

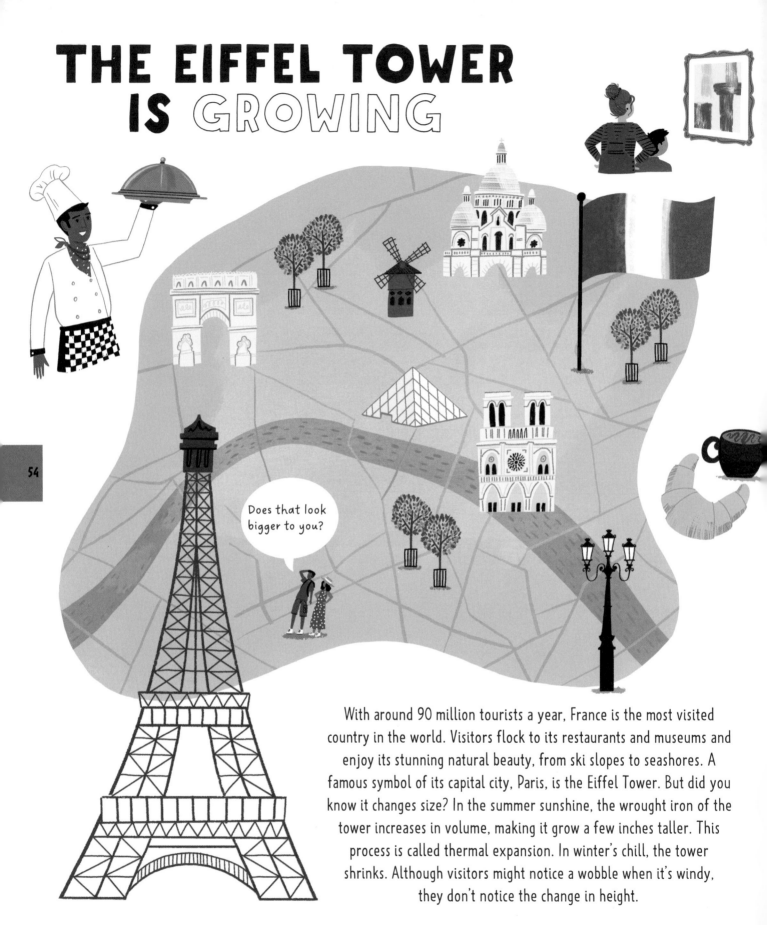

Does that look bigger to you?

With around 90 million tourists a year, France is the most visited country in the world. Visitors flock to its restaurants and museums and enjoy its stunning natural beauty, from ski slopes to seashores. A famous symbol of its capital city, Paris, is the Eiffel Tower. But did you know it changes size? In the summer sunshine, the wrought iron of the tower increases in volume, making it grow a few inches taller. This process is called thermal expansion. In winter's chill, the tower shrinks. Although visitors might notice a wobble when it's windy, they don't notice the change in height.

EVER HEARD OF A MOONBOW?

Victoria Falls, on the borders of Zimbabwe and Zambia, is one of the most beautiful places on Earth. Known as "the smoke that thunders," it is the largest sheet of falling water in the world. It is a good place to spot a moonbow—a nighttime rainbow formed when the moon's glow hits the waterfall!

We think of glaciers (rivers of ice) as icy white—but one oozes a mysterious red liquid. Taylor Glacier in Antarctica is also named "Blood Falls" for its strange, seeping red waterfalls. After years of speculation, scientists decided water from an iron-rich underground lake, long hidden by the glacier, spurts out and goes rusty red when exposed to oxygen. Or maybe there is something alive in there...

WATERFALLS OF BLOOD

CREATURE FROM THE CANYON

DON'T FEED THE SQUIRRELS

Six million years in the making, the iconic Grand Canyon in Arizona, USA, is truly a wonder. What animal do you reckon is the biggest risk to tourists there? Bighorn sheep? California condors? Gila monsters? Nope. It's a rock squirrel. Every year visitors who try to feed these small creatures are rewarded with a sharp bite.

ABANDONED ISLANDS
OF NEW YORK

New York City, USA, sometimes feels like one of the busiest places on Earth. That's not exactly true for the North and South Brother Islands, off the Bronx. In the 1850s, hospitals here treated patients with typhoid, smallpox, and tuberculosis. The infamous Mary Mallon (1869–1938), also known as "Typhoid Mary," was an Irish-American cook who may have infected over a hundred people with the disease and was confined here for two decades. Today, the islands are off-limits to the general public.

Perhaps the most densely populated place on Earth is Mong Kok in Kowloon, China. Its Chinese name means "busy corner" but that is an underestimate, as 130,000 people squish into each square kilometre! You can shop for almost anything here: there's an exotic bird market as well as entire streets dedicated to selling goldfish, trainers, and even photocopiers!

AVOID THE CRUSH!

GREAT WALL OF... RICE?

The Great Wall is an enormous chain of towers, gates, forts, and walls that has snaked through China for more than 2,300 years thanks to a secret ingredient: sticky rice. That's right! The same chewy, slightly gluey rice you enjoy eating was mixed in with the mortar (limestone and water) to bind the building materials together. Many structures in ancient China used rice in the same way.

CRATER OF FIRE

Smack in the middle of the Karakum Desert in Turkmenistan you'll find a sizzling hot, continually burning natural-gas crater sunk into the ground. No one knows how this ferocious firepit, nicknamed the "Gates of Hell," was created. It may have been set alight on purpose, to burn off toxic gas, or it may have been an industrial accident. A brave adventurer once donned a fireproof bodysuit and touched down at the bottom. They should have taken some marshmallows!

ALL TOGETHER NOW

The Serengeti National Park in Tanzania and Kenya is famous for the great migration, the world's largest movement of animals. If you happen to be in the right place at the right time, you'll bump into a whopping 1.7 million wildebeest, 500,000 zebra, and 200,000 antelope trotting along! These animals move in a giant loop throughout the year, following the rains in search of greener pastures.

EVERY YEAR **MONARCH BUTTERFLIES** MIGRATE THOUSANDS OF MILES FROM CANADA AND THE USA TO MEXICO TO **HIBERNATE** FOR THE WINTER.

THE LONGEST ANIMAL MIGRATION IN THE WORLD IS THAT OF A BIRD CALLED AN **ARCTIC TERN**. IT FLIES FROM THE ARCTIC TO THE ANTARCTIC AND BACK AGAIN EVERY YEAR!

61

THEY NEVER LEARN...

THE GREAT MIGRATION IS FRAUGHT WITH **DANGER**, AND **THOUSANDS** OF WILDEBEEST DIE ATTEMPTING IT EVERY YEAR.

RAINBOW FANTASTIC

If you love all things colorful, there are a few places that should be on your "must visit" list. Pamukkale in Turkey is a series of snowy-white structures filled with amazing blue pools of sizzling water. Australia is home to many natural wonders, but perhaps nothing so eye-popping as its flamingo-pink lakes, such as Lake Hillier. Meanwhile, hiking through rainbow-colored mountains in the Zhangye Danxia Geopark in China must feel like being in an enormous rainbow layer cake! And if you like rainbows you should also check out the Caño Cristales river in Colombia. Algae, minerals, and plants make it bloom in shockingly bright colors every year.

PAMUKKALE MEANS **"COTTON CASTLE"** IN TURKISH.

THE ALGAE THAT LIVE IN THE WATER GIVE LAKE HILLIER ITS STRIKING HUE. DON'T PACK YOUR FINS—**SWIMMING IS PROHIBITED** TO PROTECT THE CHEMICAL BALANCE OF THE WATER.

THE STRIPY ROCKS IN ZHANGYE DANXIA GEOPARK WERE CREATED BY EROSION, **VOLCANIC ACTIVITY**, AND CLIMATE CHANGE.

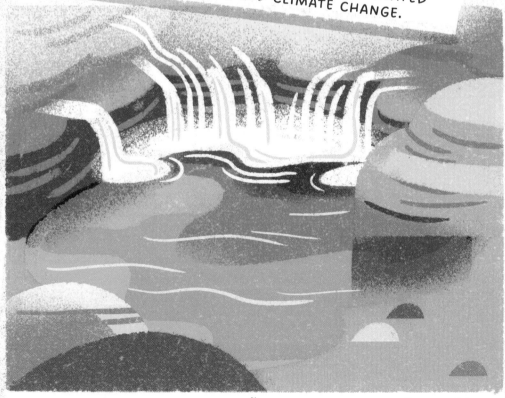

NATIVE LEGENDS SAY THE CAÑO CRISTALES RIVER **ESCAPED FROM PARADISE** TO SWIRL THROUGH THE WILDERNESS.

PURRFECT DESTINATION

Meow! There are dozens of places around the globe with more cats than people. One of the most famous is Aoshima, better known as Cat Island, in Japan. Around 20 people live here, but there are more than 120 cats! The felines were brought to this fishing island to help control the rodent population. The clowders (a group of three or more) of cats purr and prowl the island, sleeping in abandoned fishermen's cottages.

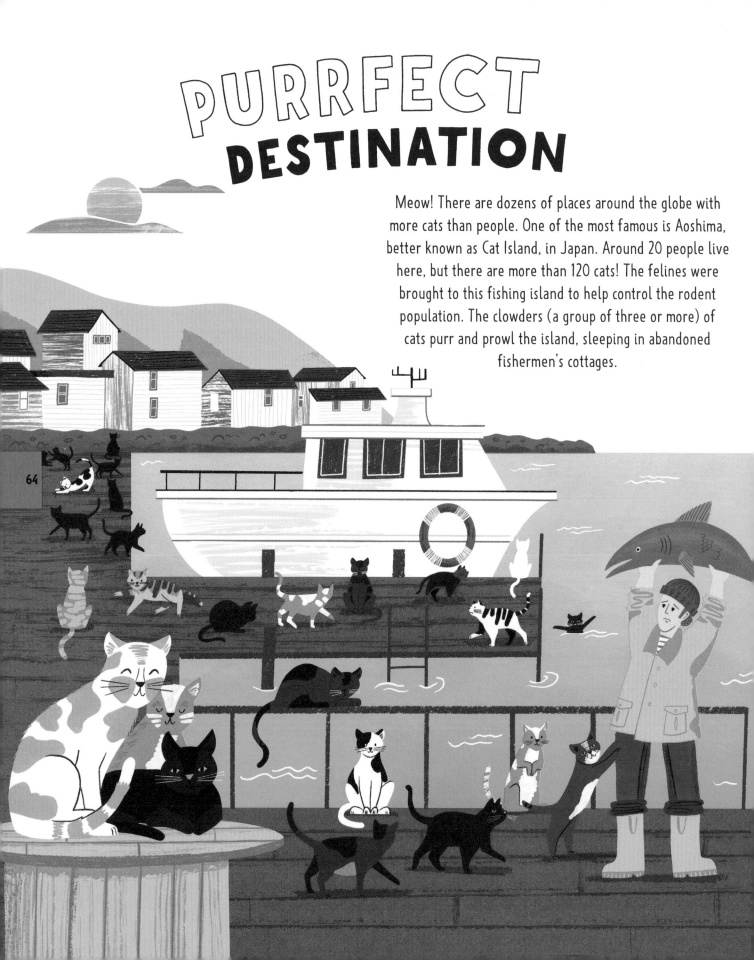

64

ALL ABOARD!

Fear of flying? Try a train. In India, around 23 million people catch a train every day. That's more than the populations of many countries! If for some reason you wanted to put all the train tracks in India into a single line, they would wrap around the Earth one and a half times. Wouldn't that be an amazing journey?

THE ISLANDS OF FEW NAMES

Where is everyone? If you want to get away from it all, consider the volcanic islands of Tristan da Cunha. This island chain, some 1,732 miles (2,787 km) from Cape Town, South Africa, is one of the most remote places on Earth. About 300 people live there—so few that there are only nine or so last names!

No, I'm here!

Mr. Green?

Over here!

PLEASE PASS THE SALT

If you want to see something truly spectacular you should take a trip to Salar de Uyuni in Bolivia. It's the world's largest salt flat. A thick crust of salt, left behind from long-evaporated rivers, stretches for more than 4,000 sq miles (10,340 sq km). When nearby lakes overflow, the water on the flats creates an amazing reflection of the sky above. It's an Instagrammer's paradise!

THE CAVE OF A MILLION LIGHTS

A cave filled with fairy lights sounds very pretty. But what if the lights were alive—thousands of tiny creatures shining in a subterranean constellation? New Zealand's Waitomo Glowworm Caves are packed with glowworms. They're not really worms, but gnat-like insects with a glowing, blue and green organ inside their tiny bodies. Glowworms use the light to attract prey, but you'll be safe on a boat tour of the cave.

When an animal can create its own light it is called bioluminescence.

NIGHT, NIGHT!

Welcome to one of the coldest, driest, and windiest places on Earth: the Amundsen-Scott South Pole Station in Antarctica. The scientists who live here watch the sun set in late summer, before living through an incredible six months of darkness. Might as well keep your pyjamas on! When the sun rises again, it is constant daytime for another six months. Would you prefer constant daytime or constant nighttime?

New York City

Singapore

DO I HAVE TIME FOR A NAP?

Buckle up! The longest nonstop commercial flight in the world is from Singapore to New York City, USA, a journey of 9,537 miles (15,348 km). In the 18 hours 50 minutes onboard, you can catch up on nine or so movies you've missed, and enjoy three meals plus snacks. The pilots and co-pilots, however, never eat the same meal, in case food poisoning (or worse) sends them all to the restroom.

If this all sounds too much for you, consider instead the shortest flight, in Scotland's Orkney Islands. It's just one and a half minutes long—barely enough time to nibble some nuts.

Orkney Islands

CHAPTER 4
USELESS PREHISTORIC KNOWLEDGE

In which the reader will learn what we can discover
from dinosaurs taking a pee, solve the case of
the mystery dinosaur-egg thief, discover why
Velociraptors aren't quite as scary as we thought,
and meet the camel with no humps.

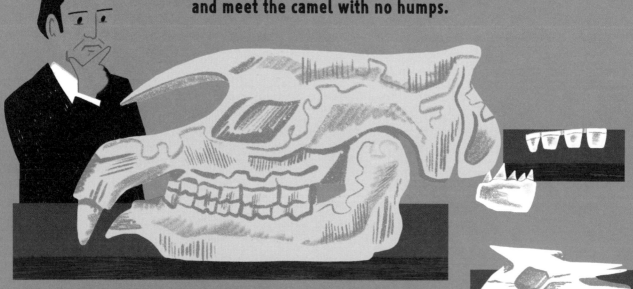

ANT FOSSIL HUNTERS

Paleontologists, scientists who study fossils, sometimes need a little help from a little insect: the humble ant. As these critters build their complex tunnels and caverns, they also pick up tiny fossils, called microfossils, and bring them to the surface. Realizing this, paleontologists started going to anthills in search of fossil treasure! Anthill fossil collecting has yielded tons of small ancient animals, including mammals, lizards, frogs, and salamanders that lived alongside giant Jurassic dinosaurs. Many new species have been found this way!

FARTS CREATED LIFE ON EARTH

Oxygen is pretty crucial for life—we breathe it all day, every day. But back in the early days of our planet, 2.4 billion years ago, there was no oxygen. So where did it come from? Look no further than cyanobacteria: bacteria that love to fart. Like plants, but way before they arrived on the scene, cyanobacteria go through a process called photosynthesis to create energy. Basically they eat sunlight to make sugar and fart out oxygen. They were so good at this that they changed the atmosphere, adding about 10 percent of the oxygen we have today! This may not seem like a lot, but it allowed plants to evolve. They created the rest of the oxygen in our atmosphere.

WE'RE GOING TO NEED A BIGGER FLYSWATTER

The largest insect to ever live? That would be Meganeuropsis. It was a type of griffinfly, a distant relative of modern dragonflies. It had a wingspan of 28 in (71 cm), similar to modern eagles! This mega-insect flew around during the Permian period, about 290 million years ago.

THE SHARK WITH A SAW IN ITS MOUTH

SHARKS DON'T HAVE SKELETONS MADE OF **BONE**. INSTEAD THEY'RE MADE OF **CARTILAGE**, LIKE OUR EARS AND THE TIPS OF OUR NOSES.

Scientists aren't exactly sure how Helicoprion used its circular saw.

You know what a shark looks like, right? Sleek, muscular, tall dorsal fin... Well, not all sharks follow the same script. In fact, one prehistoric shark looked very peculiar indeed. It's called Helicoprion, and we only know about it because we found some strange fossil spirals. The scientists were unsure if the whorls were part of a shark's snout, fins, or tail. Today they agree it was part of the lower jaw. That means this prehistoric shark had a circular saw in its mouth! Helicoprion lived about 290–270 million years ago, but the shark family is even older. In fact, sharks have been around for longer than trees!

THE PTEROSAUR AS BIG AS A PLANE

Flight is an amazing animal adaptation. Moving through the air is much more efficient than moving on land or through water. So, it is no surprise that the ability to fly has evolved multiple times over the history of our planet, whether its in insects, birds, or bats. Most things that fly today are fairly small, because it takes a lot of work to push enough air under you to lift up into the sky. This hasn't always been the case, though. Pterosaurs were prehistoric flying reptiles who ruled the skies for over 160 million years. While many pterosaurs were small, some were considerably bigger. Quetzalcoatlus was the largest animal to ever fly, with an estimated wingspan of over 33 ft (10 m). That's as big as a small plane!

CONTRARY TO POPULAR BELIEF, **PTEROSAURS AREN'T DINOSAURS.** THE WORD PTEROSAUR MEANS "WINGED REPTILE."

WHY THE LONG SCALE?

Sometimes paleontologists stumble across a fossil of an animal and it is so bizarre that they are not sure what it is! This was the case for Longisquama, a reptile found in rocks in Kyrgyzstan that dated back to the Triassic period, about 235 million years ago. While the body of the reptile looks relatively normal, it had extremely long L-shaped scales extending from its back. Until more specimens are found paleontologists cannot be sure what function these strange scales had. What do you think?

Scientists love poop, especially fossilized poop! When a poop becomes a fossil it is called a coprolite. In case you were wondering, no, they don't smell, but they are super useful. Coprolites can tell us what an animal ate, what its digestive system was like, and even how much it chewed. Fossil poop can come in all sorts of shapes, depending on the animal that made them. Sharks make spiral coprolites! Just remember: the clue is always in the poop.

PRECIOUS POOP

DON'T WORRY, DARLING, IT'S JUST A FROG

Today's amphibians, such as frogs and salamanders, are mostly cute and small, but that hasn't always been the case. If you were transported to a swamp in prehistoric Europe you could come face-to-face with the largest amphibian ever known: the mighty Mastodonsaurus! It looked like a large-headed salamander and grew more than 20 ft (6 m) long! It was an ambush predator, like today's crocodiles, and had very dense bones to help it sink to the bottom of lake beds, where it would wait for unsuspecting prey to wander by.

A CLASSIC CASE OF MISTAKEN IDENTITY

Oviraptors lived about 72 million years ago in what is Mongolia today. They walked on two legs and had large, feathered wings and a beak with no teeth. The first Oviraptor discovered was found with a pile of eggs. The paleontologists presumed this dino was stealing these eggs, so they called it Oviraptor (which means "egg thief"). Years later, more specimens were found with eggs, and even babies. It turns out that the eggs that the oviraptor was found with were their own! These dinosaurs weren't criminals but doting parents!

WANTED

THIEF!

SCIENTISTS DISCOVERED SOME OVIRAPTORS HAD **BLUE EGGS!**

WE KNOW THAT OVIRAPTORS SAT ON THEIR NESTS FOR LONG PERIODS, USING THEIR LARGE WINGS TO WARM THEIR EGGS AND **PROTECT THEIR YOUNG.** CUTIES!

TOO COOL FOR SCHOOL

Tyrannosaurus rex was one of the biggest land predators and was likely smart and fast. But when you're a large animal, it's easy to get a bit hot under the collar. T. rex's solution? It's own internal air-conditioning system! Research shows that T. rex had a lot of fat and blood vessels near the top of its head, which allowed it to push warm blood away from its brain to the surface to cool. Modern crocodiles do something similar. This amazing adaptation allowed Tyrannosaurus to hunt for longer without experiencing heat exhaustion.

Where do you think camels came from originally? Did you say the Sahara Desert in North Africa? While that is where camels are found now, the earliest known camel relative actually lived in North America 50 million years ago! It was called Protylopus, was the size of a dog, and had no hump. We know from its teeth that it liked eating leaves, and it may have stood on its hind legs to reach the juciest ones. Camels only disappeared from North America about 20,000 years ago.

NO NEED TO GET THE HUMP

VELOCIRAPTOR VS TURKEY

If you've ever seen certain Hollywood dinosaur movies, you might think that Velociraptor was one of the most fearsome prehistoric predators. Well, Hollywood doesn't always tell the truth, folks. Velociraptor was a predator, but a predator that was the same size as a turkey! It was even covered in feathers. Think less T. rex, more large chicken.

THE LESSER-KNOWN **UTAHRAPTOR** WAS ABOUT THE SIZE OF A SMALL HORSE.

THE DINO EGG SAUNA

When modern-day birds lay eggs in their nests they need to keep them warm until they hatch. The simplest way of doing this is to sit on the eggs. Dinosaurs also laid eggs, but for some of the bigger ones, sitting on the eggs wasn't possible—for obvious reasons! So how did they keep these baby dinos warm? Scientists in Argentina came across one possible explanation: some long-necked dinosaurs (sauropods) may have used geothermal vents to incubate their eggs! Geothermal vents are places where heat from the inside of the Earth bubbles up to the surface in the form of geysers or hot springs. A crafty solution, though geothermal vents aren't everywhere, so this wouldn't have worked for all sauropods.

GRAY WOLVES HAVE BEEN DOCUMENTED USING GEOTHERMAL ENERGY TO **WARM THEIR DEN.**

IN JAPAN, WILD MONKEYS CALLED **MACAQUES** BATHE IN HOT SPRINGS.

MYSTERY SPIRALS

Modern beavers build impressive dams, but that wasn't the case for their ancestors. One extinct cousin, Palaeocastor, dug deep, spiraling and complicated burrows, taller than an adult human! When these fossilized burrows were discovered in the 1890s they were called Devil's Corkscrews, and people weren't initially sure what they were. It was suggested they might be ancient plant roots, before a burrow was found with a beaver skeleton inside it!

I feel a bit dizzy...

GIANT
MAMMALS

If you thought dinosaurs were the only prehistoric giants that roamed the planet, think again. Paraceratherium was the largest non-dinosaur animal to live on land! The first fossils of this megamammal were found in Pakistan. Unfortunately, none of the fossils found were complete skeletons, so it is hard to know exactly how huge Paraceratherium was, but our best guesses suggest an animal three to four times bigger than modern-day elephants! Paraceratherium wasn't an elephant, though, but a giant hornless rhinoceros that lived between 35 and 24 million years ago.

BAT-DINO

Is it a bird? Is it a bat? No, it's a bat-like dinosaur! We now know that dinosaurs evolved the ability to fly. The evolution to flight was not a straight path, but one of experimentation, and one of these experiments involved membrane wings. Yi qi was a small Chinese dinosaur. Instead of having feathered wings, it had several long fingers with skin stretching between them, creating wings similar to the ones bats have today. Yi qi probably wasn't a great flyer, but a climber and glider who hunted bugs in the treetops.

FANCY A QUICK DIP?

There's nothing better than taking a plunge into cool water. And it turns out we're not the only ones who think so. Some dinosaurs were adapted to living at the water's edge, while others enjoyed swimming! Spinosaurus was a fearsome predator that swam using its long paddle tail, speeding underwater in pursuit of fish to eat. We've also discovered fossil tracks showing dinosaur toe marks on muddy pond bottoms— evidence that dinosaurs paddled through ponds and streams.

Amargasaurus must have been a real head-turner back in the day. It was a long-necked sauropod, but a relatively small one. It wasn't its size that made this dino stand out, though, but an unusual feature on its neck. Reaching up from its backbone were long spines. And when we say long, we mean it. These spines doubled the height of the neck! What were they there for? Some scientists think the spines created a sail-like structure, while others think they were covered with muscles. These fancy backbone spines were tallest at the neck but extended all the way down its body, making Amargasaurus a really strange-looking sauropod!

THE STRANGE SAUROPOD

SCIENTISTS USED TO BELIEVE **BRACHIOSAURUS** WAS SO BIG IT MUST HAVE LIVED IN WATER, USING ITS NOSTRILS LIKE A **SNORKEL!** ALAS, THIS WAS COMPLETELY WRONG.

THE SAUROPODS WERE BIG, BUT WHICH ONE WAS THE BIGGEST? THAT TITLE MAY BELONG TO **PATAGOTITAN**, AN ARGENTINIAN DINO 122 FT (37 M) LONG!

DIPLODOCUS HAD A TAIL EVEN LONGER THAN ITS NECK, WHICH HELPED IT TO STAY BALANCED.

WHEN YOU'VE GOT TO GO...

Any mark an animal makes can fossilize—including burrows, footprints, or even pee marks! These fossils are called trace fossils and a urolite is the name of a fossilized urine impact. If you have ever been camping or just had to go really, *really* badly, you may have seen how a stream of pee makes a dent in the soil. One of the most famous urolites was found in Brazil and was attributed to a dinosaur because of the size and the age of the rock it was found in. While we will probably never know which dinosaur made this fossil, we know it was tall and big because of how deep the trace fossil is!

KEEP IT DOWN!

For rather obvious reasons, no human has ever heard the noises a prehistoric dinosaur made, but we have some clues as to what they may have sounded like. Parasaurolophus was a duck-billed dinosaur with a tall crest. The crest was made of several bones that made hollow tubes running from each nostril. Not only did this crest look awesome (it may have been used to impress possible mates) it also amplified sounds. That's right—these dinos could honk! It is thought that these dinosaurs perhaps used these loud trumpeting noises to communicate over long distances.

Dinosaurs got old, tired bones just like your grandparents. From studying fossils we have discovered that despite being cool prehistoric beings, our dinosaur friends weren't immune to arthritis. Some of the oldest individual dinosaurs were covered in swellings around their bones at the joints, which were not found in the younger, smaller individuals of the same species. While we don't know if this was painful, we can safely assume it was uncomfortable and limited their mobility. Old dinosaurs may have struggled to get up in the mornings!

DINO-SORE!

BLOAT AND FLOAT

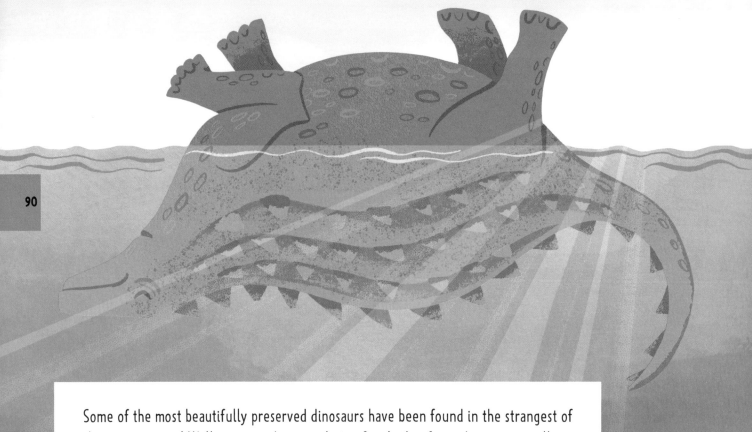

Some of the most beautifully preserved dinosaurs have been found in the strangest of places—out at sea! Well, not a modern sea, but in fossils that formed in oceans millions of years ago. How did these land-dwelling dinosaurs end up buried there, and why are they often found upside down? This is a specific type of burial called the bloat and float. What happens is, the dinosaur dies, and as it's rotting it bloats up like a balloon. If the body is washed out to sea, the bloated dinosaur floats, often upside down. This especially happened to armored dinosaurs, such as Borealopelta, which tended to flip because their heavy back plates weighed them down. Eventually the dinosaur sank to the bottom and was preserved as a fossil.

BREAKING NEWS: BIRDS ARE DINOSAURS

DINO FAMILY ALBUM

Did you know that not all dinosaurs are extinct? But don't worry, there isn't a T. rex hiding in your garden. Birds are dinosaurs! They are not only relatives of dinosaurs, they *are* a type of dinosaur that survived the extinction that wiped out the other dinosaurs. In the same way that a shark is a type of fish, a bird is a type of dinosaur. So yes, chickens and even the gulls that try to steal your ice cream are all dinosaurs.

A STING IN THE TAIL

Scorpions are not just stinging animals found in deserts, their distant relatives started out in the sea as giant sea scorpions! Sea scorpions are arthropods like spiders, bees, and shrimp. Unlike most arthropods around today, some of these sea scorpions grew to be well over 8 ft (2.5 m) long, while others grew giant snaggly claws that helped them catch slippery prey.

CHAPTER 5
USELESS HISTORY KNOWLEDGE

In which the reader will encounter a farting jester, a fearsome female pirate, the richest person in all of human history, the warrior with a knife for a hand, and some rather stinky ancient cheese.

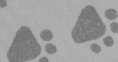

THE FISH PROTECTORS

Nervous swimmer? You're not alone. Ancient Egyptian children sometimes wore small amulets or charms in the shape of fish to protect them from harm in the water. The charms would be attached to the child's clothes or hair so they wouldn't lose them while swimming.

WHO'S LOOKING AFTER THE CHILDREN?

Neanderthals, a species of human distantly related to us, are often depicted as Stone Age idiots. But new evidence is proving that wasn't the case at all. Fossilized Neanderthal footprints from around 14 individuals, most of them children, were found at a French site called Le Rozel. These prints, dating to around 80,000 years ago, show that older Neanderthal children looked after their younger family members and that children tended to stick together in groups, likely while their parents foraged. Whether or not the kids bickered, we don't know!

You can play with my rock.

YOUR BREATH STINKS!

How do you keep your teeth clean? Maybe with some minty toothpaste? Or mouthwash? People have been trying to maintain fresh breath and white teeth for thousands of years. Their techniques were different to today, though... Some say that stale urine (that's pee to you and me) was a popular mouthwash in ancient Rome! Whether or not that's true, we're not sure, but the Romans did use pee to clean their clothes!

THIS CHARIOT **ROCKS**

The Ellora Caves, in Maharashtra, India, were carved into elaborate temples over a thousand years ago. One of these temples, dedicated to the god Shiva, contains the largest single rock carving in the world—a giant chariot. Skilled carvers started at the top of the rock and moved downward, carving out the decorated walls of the shrine as they went.

FOR SALE: MERMAIDS

Boy, she's a beauty!

In the 1800s, European sailors caught and sold mermaids. Or did they? Of course they didn't, the scoundrels. What the con artists actually did was catch skates, rays, and other similar fish, before drying them and carving them into strange little creatures called "Jenny Hanivers." They claimed that these were petrified mermaids and sold them to tourists as curiosities!

CLUES TO THE PAST

The oldest human remains in Australia, from a site called Lake Mungo, date back between 50,000 and 82,000 years ago. You may think you wouldn't be able to tell very much from a few random bones, but you'd be wrong. At that time, Australia was already an island, separated from Asia, where we know ancient humans lived. That means that humans must have built boats to cross the ocean! Another burial at Lake Mungo is the oldest known cremation, where the body of the deceased was burned to ash and then covered with a rock called ochre (which had been bashed into a powder) before being buried.

LEFTIES ASSEMBLE

Are you right-handed or left-handed? Evidence from skeletal remains shows that Neanderthals (our extinct cousins) and Homo sapiens (that's us) had about the same percentages of right-handed and left-handed people in their populations. They were more similar to us than you might think!

THE CLUE IS IN THE POOP

The 1803 Lewis and Clark Expedition saw a few individuals explore the western half of North America. Along the way they learned about the geography and wildlife of the continent and encountered many of the Indigenous tribes that called it home. But that's not all that happened. The people on the 1803 Lewis and Clark Expedition also took laxative pills! They were laced with so much mercury that traces of where they went to the bathroom can still be detected by chemical analysis. Researchers have tracked the stops along the expedition's route thanks to the mercury in that 200-year-old poop!

THE EXPEDITION WAS COMMISSIONED BY PRESIDENT THOMAS JEFFERSON. ONE OF THE REASONS HE SENT THE TEAM WEST WAS TO TRY TO FIND LIVING **HERDS OF MASTODONS** (PREHISTORIC ELEPHANT-LIKE MAMMALS). THEY DIDN'T FIND ANYTHING, BECAUSE MASTODONS ARE PREHISTORIC.

MERIWETHER LEWIS AND WILLIAM CLARK WERE AIDED IN THEIR EXPEDITION BY A SHOSHONE TEENAGER CALLED **SACAGAWEA**.

WILLIAM CLARK TOOK AN ENSLAVED MAN CALLED **YORK** ON THE TRIP. YORK WAS VITAL TO THE SUCCESS OF THE EXPEDITION, BUT DIDN'T RECEIVE THE CREDIT HE WAS DUE UNTIL AFTER HE DIED.

ONE LINCOLN SPECIAL, COMING UP

If you dig a little, you'll find that most people have an interesting past. Abraham Lincoln, the 16th president of the USA, is known for winning the US Civil War and ending slavery in the country. What a lot of people don't realize was that in his early years he was an elite wrestler and licensed bartender!

A woman named Hatshepsut ruled from 1479–1458 BCE as one of the few female pharaohs in ancient Egyptian history. She had a successful military career, expanded Egypt's trade networks, and was memorialized in art and sculpture in the traditional male form of a pharaoh. Haven't heard of her? You're not alone. Her role in history wasn't well known until around 100 years ago, because after her death her successors erased her name from most of her monuments and art.

THE SECRET LEGEND OF THE FEMALE PHARAOH

A PIRATE'S LIFE FOR ME

Between 1795 and 1810, a woman named Ching Shih was the most fearsome pirate in Chinese waters. She enforced a strict and brutal code of law over her fleet of ships, eventually amassing around 1,200 ships with 70,000 sailors—eight times bigger than the legendary Spanish Armada! She also cleverly negotiated with the Chinese Imperial Navy to ensure that any of her pirates could retire from a life of crime and rejoin society. This made her specific type of piracy quite respectable. The retired pirates probably had some good stories to tell their grandchildren!

TIME TO COME OUT OF YOUR SHELL

In the Bronze Age of the Mediterranean, around 5,000 years ago, anyone who was anyone was seen in purple clothes. *How did they make purple clothes that long ago?* I hear you ask. Well, the color came from smooshed-up sea-snail mucus! The dye was exorbitantly expensive because of the labor and sheer number of snails needed to make a single batch. Fashion, eh?

THE SECRET OF THE BEANS

If you like vanilla-flavored ice cream you have Edmond Albius to thank. Vanilla beans, where vanilla flavor comes from, could only be found and gathered in the wild until 1841. This was because up until then vanilla plants were pollinated by a single species of bee. However, Edmond, an enslaved boy on the island of Réunion in the Indian Ocean, figured out how to pollinate the flowers artificially. So great was his method, which involves a blade of grass and a thumb, that it's still used today!

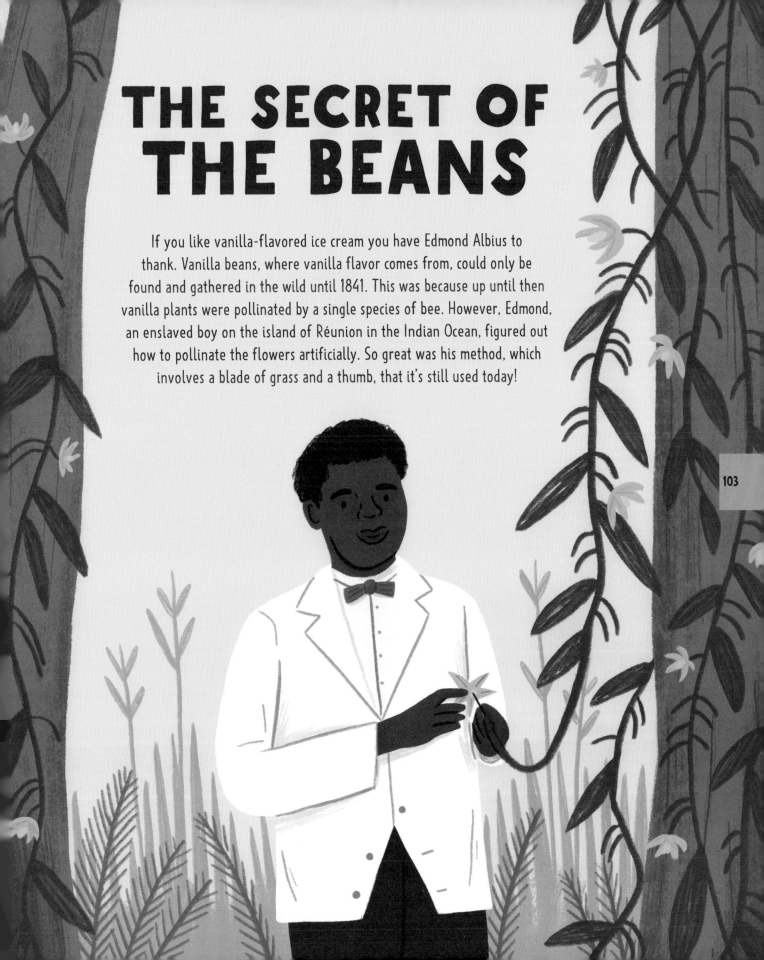

THERE SHE BLOWS

In 1628, Sweden launched a ship named the *Vasa*. She was a huge, ornate warship riddled with cannons, a mighty vessel if ever there was one. Alas, she was so top-heavy and poorly designed that just 4,265 ft (1,300 m) into her maiden voyage she was blown over by a gust of wind and sank! The *Vasa* was initially designed to hold 36 massive brass cannons. However, the king, who was less of an engineer than one would hope in this situation, ordered that she be outfitted with 64 cannons. The water at the bottom of the ocean where the *Vasa* sank was very cold and didn't contain much oxygen. The little marine worms that love to eat up shipwrecks couldn't survive there, so 95 percent of the ship was still perfectly intact when the wreckage was raised in 1961!

I can see land!

IT'S BELIEVED BY SAILORS THAT SMASHING A **BOTTLE OF CHAMPAGNE** AGAINST THE HULL OF A SHIP BEFORE ITS MAIDEN VOYAGE BRINGS IT GOOD LUCK.

THE MOST FAMOUS SHIP TO SINK ON ITS MAIDEN VOYAGE WAS THE *TITANIC*. IT CRASHED INTO AN **ICEBERG** IN 1912 ON ITS WAY TO NEW YORK FROM ENGLAND.

IF YOU'RE EVER IN STOCKHOLM YOU CAN HEAD TO THE **VASA MUSEUM** AND SEE THE SHIP FOR YOURSELF!

WHAT A STINK!

Have you ever found a bit of cheese in a fridge that is really starting to stink the place out? Spare a thought for the archaeologists investigating a burial chamber in China. They came across cheese that dates to around 3,600 years ago. Not only that, but it was located on the bodies of mummies!

KA-CHING!

On a pilgrimage to Mecca in 1324 CE, Mansa Musa, king of the Mali Empire, brought so much money with him that his visit caused the economies of the region to utterly collapse! It took 12 years for them to recover. It's no wonder that Mansa Musa is considered to be the richest person who ever lived.

MEET THE HELLFIGHTERS

An infantry regiment of the United States National Guard, consisting mainly of Black soldiers, was one of the first African-American regiments to serve in the First and Second World Wars. The men of the regiment bravely fought for their country, despite the fact that they faced racial discrimination back home. According to popular legend, the German army named them Hellfighters. These men spent more time in the frontline trenches of both World Wars than any other American unit.

THERE'S A BIT OF SHELL IN MY DINNER

Head to a fancy restaurant in Paris and you might spot snails on the menu. This is no recent phenomenon. In fact, ancient Romans raised snails for food and fed them on grains and herbs so they would be extra tasty!

THE ANCIENT SUPERHERO

What do you do if you're a warrior, but you lose your hand in battle? One man had an ingenious idea... He was a Lombard warrior—one of the Germanic tribes that ruled the region of Italy around the eighth century CE. He was found in a 1,400-year-old tomb in Italy with a knife fitted where his hand used to be! What a handy accessory! Fighting was easier; presumably brushing his teeth was a little harder.

ROYAL PROTECTORS

The Kingdom of Dahomey (modern-day Benin in Africa) had an all-female military regiment that protected the royal family from the 1600s to the late 1800s. These fearsome warriors undertook intense physical exercise to keep in tip-top shape, were conditioned to withstand pain, and were not allowed to marry or have children. The trade-off was they were wealthy and had very high status in the community.

ROLAND THE FARTER

The court minstrel (a type of medieval entertainer) to the English King Henry II was named Roland the Farter. Guess what his big talent was? That's right—while the royal trumpeters were trumpeting, so was Roland. He performed his special farty dance every Christmas for the king and his court. Hopefully it didn't put them off their dinner.

ANCIENT NOODLES

The oldest preserved noodles in the world were found in a small clay bowl in a 4,000-year-old village site in China. Pretty cool! You may be wondering how they came to be in such good condition? Well, a massive flood brought so much sediment into the village that everything was quickly covered, keeping it preserved for thousands of years!

PRUNE, MY DEAR?

In Elizabethan England, around the same time that Shakespeare was jotting down his best plays, prunes were all the rage. If you wanted to court a pretty girl, you bought her some stewed prunes.

MODERN HOUSE CATS DESCENDED FROM A SPECIES CALLED THE **AFRICAN WILDCAT.**

ANCIENT EGYPTIANS REVERED CATS. MANY CATS WERE **MUMMIFIED** BY THEIR OWNERS AFTER THEY DIED!

CATS LIVED ALONGSIDE HUMANS IN CHINA MORE THAN **5,000 YEARS AGO.**

HERE, KITTY!

113

Cats, you gotta love them. Throughout history these kitties have been up to mischief. Cat pawprints have been found on multiple historic surfaces, from ancient Roman clay tiles (stepped on when wet) to 15th-century manuscripts (inky paws left a trail). In 1420, one medieval monk found that the manuscript he had been working on had been peed on in the night by a feline visitor, and so he scribbled next to the wet spot!

CHAPTER 6

USELESS CULTURE KNOWLEDGE

In which the reader will hang out at a scrambled egg festival, learn about the dolphin that haunts a theater, boogie with some animals, and find out if it's possible to eat a building.

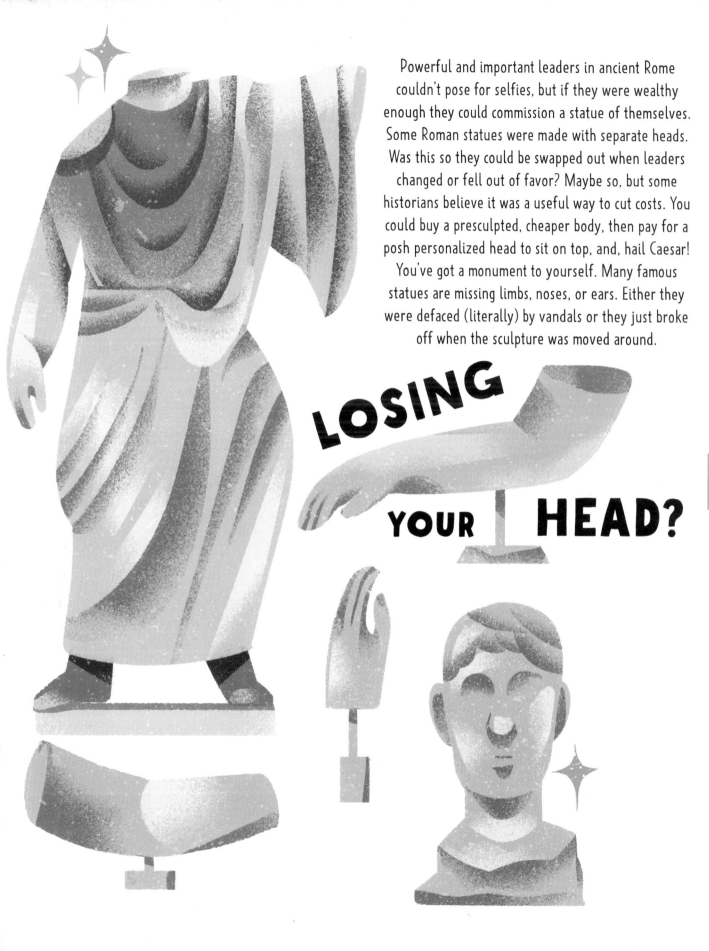

Powerful and important leaders in ancient Rome couldn't pose for selfies, but if they were wealthy enough they could commission a statue of themselves. Some Roman statues were made with separate heads. Was this so they could be swapped out when leaders changed or fell out of favor? Maybe so, but some historians believe it was a useful way to cut costs. You could buy a presculpted, cheaper body, then pay for a posh personalized head to sit on top, and, hail Caesar! You've got a monument to yourself. Many famous statues are missing limbs, noses, or ears. Either they were defaced (literally) by vandals or they just broke off when the sculpture was moved around.

LOSING YOUR HEAD?

AN EGG-CELLENT FESTIVAL

To celebrate springtime, citizens of Zenica in the eastern European country of Bosnia and Herzegovina hold a festival called Čimburijada. They meet up at sunrise near the Bosna River and scramble hundreds of eggs in enormous pans! Scrambled egg lovers from all over join this bountiful breakfast to welcome warmer weather. No one is exactly sure how this yolky tradition started, but the eggs symbolize new life and exciting times in the year ahead.

IF EGGS AREN'T YOUR THING YOU COULD JOIN ONE OF THE LARGEST FOOD FIGHTS IN ITALY. JUST BEFORE EASTER, RESIDENTS OF **IVREA** TEAM UP TO BOMBARD EACH OTHER WITH **FLYING ORANGES!**

IF THAT'S NOT JUICY ENOUGH, TRY THE MASSIVE TOMATO FIGHT AT THE FESTIVAL **LA TOMATINA**, HELD IN THE TOWN OF BUÑOL, SPAIN, AT THE END OF AUGUST.

PAWS FOR THOUGHT

Did the dog eat your homework? How about the first draft of your famous novel? American author John Steinbeck's original manuscript of his future classic *Of Mice and Men* was shredded by his dog, Toby. About two months of writing became confetti at the paws of his pooch. Steinbeck thought Toby might have been giving him a bad review.

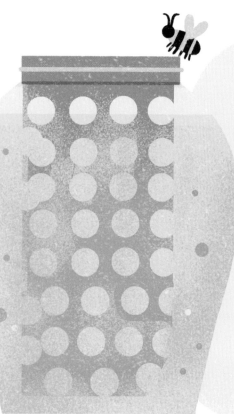

ANCIENT HONEY

Did you know honey can last up to 3,000 years? Archaeologists digging out a tomb in Egypt found an ancient stash of honey, and it was perfectly edible. Because honey contains so much sugar and so little water, it's hard for bacteria to grow in it. Honey was popular in ancient Egypt—it was even used to treat diseases!

THE PAINTER PRODIGY

The incredible Spanish painter Pablo Picasso (1881–1973) could draw before he could talk, and when he *did* talk, his first spoken word was "pencil." When Picasso was just 13, his father, an art teacher, threw up his hands and gave all of his art materials to his vastly more talented son. Many of Picasso's works are among the most valuable in the world, and along with Vincent van Gogh and Andy Warhol, he dominates the lists of best-selling paintings. About his own skills, Picasso once said, "It has taken me my whole life to learn to draw like a child."

No actor wants to hear a crowd boo, but they are even more wary of the countless ghosts that are said to haunt the world's stages. These spirits get up to all kinds of mischief: making weird giggles, creating a sudden chill, or moving props around. London's Peacock Theatre is supposedly haunted by a dolphin, however that happened. It's a tradition in theaters around the world that the last person out the door at night must leave a single light on for the ghosts.

HAUNTED THEATERS

Experts think the very oldest form of art was most likely painting. You won't see this art framed in a museum. Instead, it is etched (scratched) or painted on the walls of dark caves, on bones, or rock formations. Perhaps the oldest art discovered so far is a 45,500-year-old cave wall drawing of three small pigs (no, not THE three little pigs) in Indonesia. No one is telling fibs, but it depends what you count as art. The pigs are representational art, meaning the drawings look like, well, pigs. There may be nonrepresentational art, such as signs and symbols, that is older. But the discovery of the pigs was enough to make the experts squeal.

THE PIG MASTERPIECE

It looks nothing like me!

121

FANCY A CHAT?

Shikamoo

Bonjour

As-salam

Namaste

Guten tag

Hello

Nei Ho

There are more than 7,000 languages spoken in the 197 countries of the world, although the numbers change constantly. Half of the world's population speak only 0.3 percent of languages— including Mandarin, Spanish, English, Hindi, and Arabic. Some 2,000 languages are only spoken by less than 1,000 people each, some by only a handful. UNESCO (United Nations Educational, Scientific and Cultural Organization) monitors languages at risk of disappearing.

THE BOOK OF GOLD

What's the oldest book in the world? It depends on what you call a book. You may be holding one now, but what if you are reading from a clay tablet, or a paper scroll? Words handwritten by monks, or scrolling on a screen? Bound together, or loose sheets? The winner may be the Etruscan Gold Book, made from six sheets of gold held together with rings. Found in a canal in Bulgaria, the 2,673-year-old gold plates show horses and soldiers as well as words. Imagine the library fine if it were overdue!

HOW DOES MY LOINCLOTH LOOK?

The ultimate in vintage fashion is the loincloth, perhaps the oldest item of clothing. This rectangle of fabric was wrapped around the waist several times and tied or belted to keep it closed. Some very fancy types hung ornaments and trinkets from the waist. The next big fashion smash was the skirt, worn by both women and men. Just like today, skirts came in lengths from mini to maxi.

SWEET CASH

Ever eaten a chocolate coin? Nothing new there. The ancient Maya civilization (250–900 CE) of Central America used cacao beans, the main ingredient in chocolate, as a form of money. Cups of tasty hot chocolate even appeared in their art. When the cacao tree crop failed, the whole civilization suffered.

MIGHTY DANCERS

Be careful when shaking hands with a ballet dancer. They have an incredibly strong grip. In fact, many tests show a professional ballet dancer is often fitter and stronger than other types of athlete. They can lift 2.5 times their body weight! Ballerinas are true superheroes. And like superheroes, they also wear tights.

LATE-NIGHT CAVE RAVE

So how long have people been dancing? Indian cave paintings of dancers date back to 8,000 BCE. Some of these dances were probably part of religious ceremonies, while others were for celebrations. People also danced just to let their hair down and have fun. Many dancers in the paintings wore animal heads: donkeys, bulls, monkeys, and crocodiles were popular dance hats. One of the most unusual of these dance paintings is of a dancing cow having a pee.

WHAT'S THAT SOUND?

Sound effects geniuses make noises for Hollywood in all sorts of clever ways. Two cups rubbed together have created an otherworldly scream. Crushed walnuts stood in for a broken neck, and paper slid out of an envelope created the whoosh of spaceship doors. A dinosaur's sneeze was a mix of a whale's blowhole and a fire hose turning on! One of the most famous sound effects is the Wilhelm scream. This sound, of an actor pretending to be bitten by an alligator, was recorded in 1951 and has appeared in countless famous movies and video games.

A SMASHING GOOD TIME

A smashing custom is the Polterabend, in Germany. The night before a wedding, friends and family gather near the bride or groom's home and smash china cups, bowls, plates, flowerpots, tiles—even toilets and sinks. The broken shards are believed to bring good luck to the couple. Smashing glass is a Jewish wedding tradition, and since ancient Roman times, newlyweds have smushed cake onto themselves or each other, or tossed it overhead to wish for a happy married life.

SNEAKY BY NAME, SNEAKY BY NATURE

Sneakers got their name because people could sneak around without being heard wearing them. These rubber-soled shoes first appeared sometime around the 18th century. In 1917, Marquis Converse made sneakers just for playing basketball, called Converse All Stars. These cool kicks have snuck onto the list of the best-selling basketball shoes of all time.

PEANUT DYNAMITE

You might make a dynamite peanut butter and jelly sandwich, but did you know peanuts can make actual dynamite? Peanut oil makes glycerol, an ingredient of nitroglycerin. This is in the explosive recipe for dynamite. Don't worry, though—other ingredients are way more commonly used and it's perfectly safe to eat peanut butter!

THE ANIMAL DISCO

Animals like music, but maybe not your favorite bands. They respond to species-specific sounds that match their own vocal styles and scales, just like we do. With the science of zoomusicology, researchers test out tunes written just for wolves, whales, birds, cats, and monkeys, to see how they respond. Monkeys were quiet during slow, sad songs but swung around like monkeys do during fast numbers!

INSECTS CALLED **CICADAS** SING BY VIBRATING PARTS OF THEIR BODIES. THEY DO THIS TO ATTRACT MATES.

BIRDS ARE PERHAPS THE BEST ANIMAL MUSICIANS. **MOZART** HAD A STARLING THAT COULD COPY HIS GREATEST HITS!

WHALES USE **WHALE SONG** TO COMMUNICATE WITH EACH OTHER OVER VAST DISTANCES.

129

THE BOOK-SNIFFERS

Do you like to sniff books? If not, give it a go right now and see what you think. Bibliosmia is the act of smelling books. A book's distinctive smell is created when the paper, ink, and glue in it decays (goes off) and releases smelly chemicals. As soon as a book is made, it starts to decay, and that's what we are sniffing.

HAVE YOU EVER SEEN A LION DANCE?

If you visit a Chinese New Year's parade, you might see (and certainly hear) the colorful, loud spectacle of dancers operating huge puppet-like lions. The Lion Dance began in the Han Dynasty (206 BCE–220 CE) to chase away evil and bring good fortune. Some lions act like big cats, and others perform acrobatic tricks as they parade to the banging of drums (to represent the lion's heartbeat) and hissing fireworks (to scare off nasties). Lions nibble on lettuce because it looks like money, then spit salad back over the crowd to spread the wealth. You might even be on the menu—a lion might stop to playfully nibble someone in the crowd!

THE WEIGHT OF IT ALL

The internet is vast, enormous, gigantic, and just plain huge. Can you think of even one area of your life the internet does not touch? Yet how much would it weigh, if that were possible? Physicist Russell Seitz wanted to work it out. He concluded it was all about electrons—electrically charged particles found inside atoms. Any storage and transfer of information depends on electrons, and they have a tiny amount of weight. Doing the complicated math, he proposed that the entire internet weighs about 2 oz (60 g)—about the same as a tennis ball!

COULD YOU
EAT A BUILDING?

A gingerbread house, maybe, but how about a house you can live in? Since the Hanging Gardens of Babylon in 600 BCE, buildings and plants have existed together. We grow all kinds of plants on rooftops, balconies, windowsills, and walls. The next step may be creating edible homes and furniture. In Japan, researchers have turned food waste like onion skins, misshapen vegetables, and coffee grounds into building materials, and built a house from cabbage and fruit peel!

MOZART OUTSELLS BEYONCÉ

THE BEST-SELLING
BAND OF ALL TIME
IS BRITISH BAND
THE BEATLES.

It's so easy—just tap an app, stream, and sing along. It seems impossible to think that back in the day, if you wanted to hear music, you had to make it yourself or find someone who could. American inventor Thomas Edison first recorded the words "Mary had a little lamb" on a replayable wax tube in 1877, and the history of recorded music began. In 1903, wealthy people could buy record players and early recordings of classical music. Vinyl records arrived in 1948. So did new rock and pop stars take over from the old-school crowd? Surprisingly, no. In the USA, "old" music (at least 18 months old but typically much older) represents about 70 percent of total sales. In 2016, Wolfgang Amadeus Mozart sold more CDs than Beyoncé!

135

ART USED TO BE AN OLYMPIC SPORT

On your marks, set, paint! Did you know that the arts, like painting, sculpture, architecture, literature, and music, used to be Olympic events? You might imagine people dressed in berets and smocks dragging their canvases and easels around a running track, dripping paint along the way. But this wasn't quite the case. From 1912 to 1952, Olympic judges gave medals to artists who showed excellence in sport-themed art. More than 150 medals were awarded to these artistic champions.

FORGET GOLD MEDALS—ONE OLYMPIC HERO, A NORWEGIAN COACH WHO ASSISTED THE CANADIAN TEAM, WAS REWARDED WITH 7,400 **TINS OF MAPLE SYRUP.** SWEET!

CHAPTER 7

USELESS SCIENCE KNOWLEDGE

In which the reader will find out why rollercoasters have medicinal benefits, learn why you should never touch Marie Curie's notebooks, wonder whether bread caused a bout of witchcraft, and discover what their smelly farts have in common with volcanoes!

IT'S POSSIBLE TO WALK ON CUSTARD

As well as being ABSOLUTELY DELICIOUS, custard is what's known as a non-Newtonian fluid. If you didn't know already (and I don't blame you) this means that it can behave like both a liquid and a solid! If you try to walk on a normal liquid, such as water, you'll sink to the bottom pretty quickly as your foot pushes apart the particles that make up the liquid. With non-Newtonian fluids however, rather than moving apart when pressure is applied, the particles lock together, behaving like a solid for a moment. But, if you want to stay on top of the custard, you'll have to keep moving—if you stop, you'll sink!

APPLE OR ONION?

138

Have you ever had a cold and found that everything tastes a bit different? This is because our sense of smell is a really important part of how we taste things (in fact, scientists estimate that 80 percent of taste is actually smell). Apples and onions may seem nothing like each other, but they contain a lot of the same flavor chemicals, so our tongues alone can't tell them apart. Fortunately, when we bite into an apple or an onion, they release different scent molecules, so our noses can figure out which one is which. This means that without a sense of smell, apples and onions taste the same!

Why is this apple making me cry?!

RAIN VS SNOW

Usually, we expect the particles in a solid (like snow) to be very close together and the particles in a liquid (like rain) to be a bit farther apart. But for water and ice, things are a bit weird and it's the other way around. So, unlike water, ice is full of empty space. That means that when water freezes, it gets bigger. In fact, weather scientists estimate that 1 in (2.5 cm) of rain would become 10 in (25 cm) of snow!

THE FASTEST TRAIN IN THE WORLD
FLOATS
ABOVE THE TRACK

The Japanese bullet train travels at a mind-blowing 375 mph (604 kph)! It may look like any other train from the outside, but hidden in the wheels and the track are a series of powerful electromagnets. Once the train reaches 93 mph (150 kph), these magnets are activated and the magnetic force is strong enough to lift the train 4 in (10 cm) above the ground! When it's floating, the train doesn't have any friction with the track, so it can go much faster than normal.

THE BULLET TRAIN'S AERODYNAMIC NOSE WAS INSPIRED BY A **KINGFISHER'S BEAK.**

THE FIRST COMPUTER FILLED A
WHOLE ROOM

It's hard to imagine, but computers have only been around for just over 80 years. The first complete digital computer was called ENIAC (Electronic Numerical Integrator and Computer) and was built by the American military to solve complex calculations. Made up of thousands of vacuum tubes and other bulky electronic parts, this huge machine was almost 100 ft (30 m) long and used as much power as 30,000 light bulbs! But despite its huge size, ENIAC only had enough memory for about 20 words at a time.

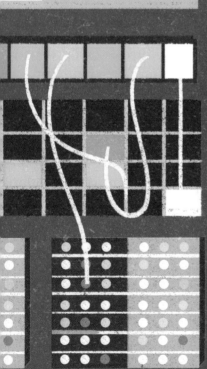

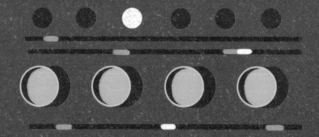

ENIAC WAS SO BIG IT
WEIGHED A WHOPPING
27 TONS!

THE FIRST COMPUTER
PROGRAM WAS WRITTEN BY A
19TH-CENTURY WOMAN CALLED
ADA LOVELACE. SHE WAS THE
DAUGHTER OF THE FAMOUS
POET LORD BYRON.

THE **FIRST COMPUTER
MOUSE** WAS INVENTED
BY ENGINEERS DOUGLAS
ENGELBART AND BILL ENGLISH
AND WAS MADE OF WOOD!

141

SAY CHEESE!

Up until 1827, the only way to get a picture was to paint it. This wouldn't do for French inventor Joseph Nicéphore Niépce, who wanted to find a way to capture pictures more quickly. He used a clever device called a camera obscura to reflect light into a little box, creating a miniature version of the image inside. He then covered a sheet of pewter in a mixture of bitumen (a sticky black liquid that comes from gasoline) and lavender oil and left it in the box. After several days, the light shining on this mixture made it harden, and Niépce had the first black-and-white photograph!

WON'T BE MUCH LONGER!

SHOULD HAVE TAKEN A CALCULATOR?

Technology moves so quickly. Back in 1962, NASA engineers designed a state-of-the-art computer for the Apollo 11 moon mission, but by the time the rocket was ready for launch in 1969, this computer was already slightly out of date! The Apollo 11 Guidance Computer had a total of 32,768 bits of memory, equivalent to about two pages of text, and helped the astronauts navigate to the moon. Incredibly, calculators released in the 1990s had 32 times this amount of memory and processed information almost 350 times faster!

THIS WILL SEND YOU TO SLEEP

Doctors use drugs called anesthestics to send patients to sleep before operating on them. The amazing thing is, no one knows how they work! This problem has been puzzling scientists for over 200 years. The brain is phenomenally complicated and we're only just beginning to understand it. There seem to be hundreds or even thousands of chemical reactions controlling whether we are awake or asleep, so working out what an anesthetic is doing is a big challenge! Interestingly, scientists have discovered that anesthestics also send plants to sleep, so it might not have anything to do with the brain at all.

SEARCHING FOR THE PHILOSOPHER'S STONE

Back in the 1600s, scientists were obsessed with trying to discover the philosopher's stone—a mythical substance that was said to turn metal to gold! Hennig Brand was a German alchemist and in 1669 he collected pee from his neighbors and boiled it until it turned into a black sludge. He then heated this horrible gunk, added sand, and purified the mucky mixture. One of the new substances he made as a result of his unusual experiment was a white solid that glowed in the dark. Brand named it phosphorus. He may not have created the philosopher's stone, but he became the first person to discover a new chemical element!

Atoms are the building blocks that make up everything, including you. But did you know that atoms themselves are made up of even smaller particles? Right in the center is the nucleus, a miniscule cluster of particles called protons and neutrons. Whizzing around outside of this are some even smaller particles called electrons. But separating the nucleus from the electrons is a huge area of nothingness! In fact, if you imagine the atom is the size of a football pitch, the nucleus would only be the size of a marble. That means you're mostly empty space!

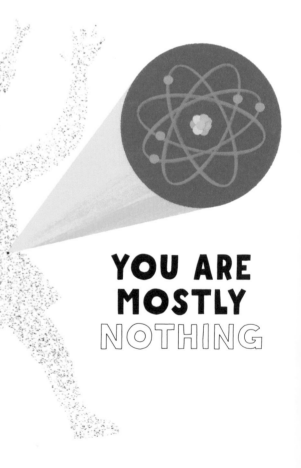

YOU ARE MOSTLY NOTHING

YOU ARE 13.8 BILLION YEARS OLD

Well, sort of. All of the hydrogen atoms in your body were created in the Big Bang, 13.8 billion years ago. In fact, all the hydrogen in the universe was created in the Big Bang! In the very first moments after this massive explosion, the universe was too hot for atoms to exist, but billions and trillions of even smaller particles were created. Once everything had cooled down a little, these tiny particles combined to make the first atoms, starting with the simplest—hydrogen. Since then, the universe has been using small hydrogen atoms to make bigger and more complicated chemicals. But until we have another Big Bang, it won't be able to make any more hydrogen. You might need a few more candles on your birthday cake next year...

TEACHING CARS
TO BEHAVE THEMSELVES

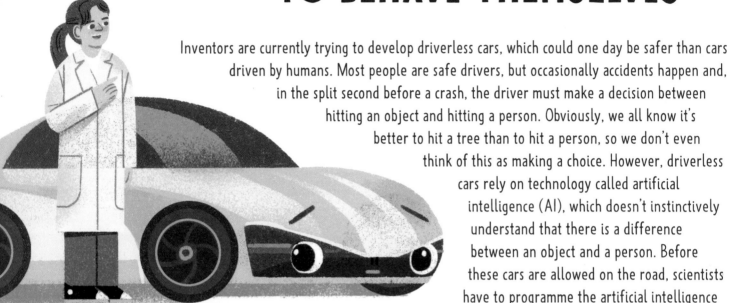

Inventors are currently trying to develop driverless cars, which could one day be safer than cars driven by humans. Most people are safe drivers, but occasionally accidents happen and, in the split second before a crash, the driver must make a decision between hitting an object and hitting a person. Obviously, we all know it's better to hit a tree than to hit a person, so we don't even think of this as making a choice. However, driverless cars rely on technology called artificial intelligence (AI), which doesn't instinctively understand that there is a difference between an object and a person. Before these cars are allowed on the road, scientists have to programme the artificial intelligence so that it can learn right from wrong!

HOW DO YOU LIKE YOUR EGG?

Do you know it's possible to unboil an egg? Eggs are full of proteins: long complicated molecules that are carefully wrapped up like a ball of string. When you boil an egg, the heat causes these molecules to unravel and the strings of protein become knotted together, making the egg solid. But scientists have found a way to reverse this reaction! They inject a boiled egg with a chemical called urea, then spin it terrifically fast (5,000 times per minute) to separate the tangled protein strings. Unfortunately, urea is one of the main components of pee, so you probably wouldn't want to eat the egg afterward!

When we eat, we aren't just swallowing food but quite a lot of air as well. All this trapped gas has to get out somehow and most people fart between 10 and 20 times a day. Usually, this is all sound and no stink, but sometimes the good bacteria in your digestive system produce a particularly smelly gas called hydrogen sulphide from breaking down foods like egg and fish. This stinky substance is the same noxious gas produced by volcanoes! In fact, volcanologists monitor it to detect volcanic activity.

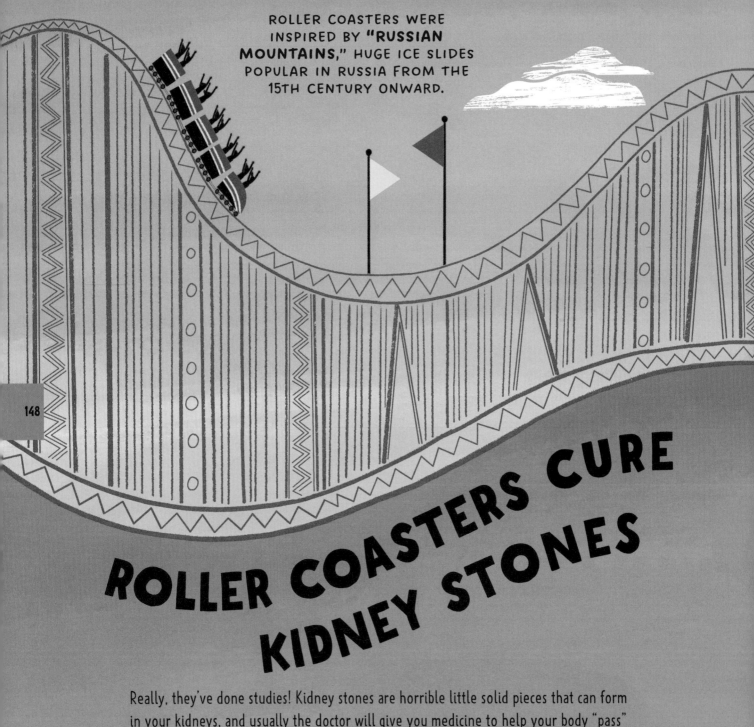

ROLLER COASTERS WERE INSPIRED BY **"RUSSIAN MOUNTAINS,"** HUGE ICE SLIDES POPULAR IN RUSSIA FROM THE 15TH CENTURY ONWARD.

ROLLER COASTERS CURE KIDNEY STONES

Really, they've done studies! Kidney stones are horrible little solid pieces that can form in your kidneys, and usually the doctor will give you medicine to help your body "pass" these stones when you go to the toilet. However, in the USA several people said riding on the Thunder Mountain roller coaster at Disney World cured their kidney stones without medicine. A team of scientists were very interested in these strange claims and 3D-printed a kidney to test the theory. Surprisingly, their experiment not only confirmed these rumors but also revealed that sitting at the back was best!

THE FIRST ROLLER COASTER WAS THE **PROMENADES-AÉRIENNES** ("THE AERIAL WALK") IN PARIS, FRANCE. IT OPENED IN 1817.

149

YOU MUST BE THIS TALL

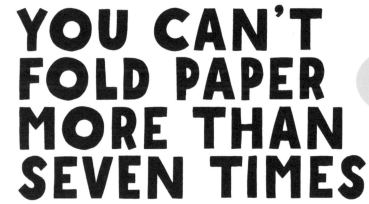
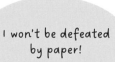

YOU CAN'T FOLD PAPER MORE THAN SEVEN TIMES

I won't be defeated by paper!

Go on, give it a try! It gets surprisingly tough very quickly, doesn't it? We can actually explain why this is the case using some fairly simple math. When you fold a piece of paper, you take something that is one layer thick and make it two layers thick. But when you fold it a second time, you take something that is two layers thick and make it four layers thick! Folding a third time will make eight layers, four folds will be sixteen, and so on. Each time, you're doubling the number of layers, so by the time you have folded it seven times, you have a whopping 128 layers and it's impossible to fold it any more.

YOU CAN START A FIRE WITH WATER

Which sounds kind of strange as we'd usually use water to put out a fire! But there's a group of elements called the alkali metals that react incredibly violently with water! The reaction makes a new chemical called a metal hydroxide and gives out so much heat that the metal itself catches fire. Hydrogen gas is also formed and, in some cases, is produced so quickly that it causes an explosion!

DEATH BY FASHION!

During the Victorian era (1837–1901) in the United Kingdom, more and more people could afford new clothes because of the riches they had made during the Industrial Revolution. With this new-found access to fashion, Victorians wanted bolder and brighter colours and were willing to pay any price to get them. Unfortunately the exotic new dyes created by scientists hid a terrible secret – many of them were made using toxic metals such as arsenic and chromium! When the fashionable ladies and gentlemen wore their magnificent new clothes, small amounts of these poisons were absorbed through their skin, causing all sorts of unfortunate side effects. The price of fashion, eh darling?

Humans have been using reflective surfaces to look at themselves for thousands of years! Alas, the first mirrors only reflected things in black and white. The Aztecs polished a type of black volcanic rock called obsidian, creating a glassy surface that could reflect just enough light to see a version of yourself. The mystic and ethereal images that appeared in the stone earned obsidian the title "smoking mirror," and it became the symbol of Tezcatlipoca, the Aztec god of sorcery.

MIRROR, MIRROR ON THE ROCK

FRIDGES CAN HEAT UP A ROOM

Fridges work by circulating a coolant through metal coils inside and outside of the fridge. Starting on the inside as a liquid, the coolant absorbs heat from the food to keep it cool. This heat turns the coolant into a gas, which then flows through the metal coils on the outside of the fridge, releasing the heat into the room. But when you leave the door open, the fridge has to work much harder to try and cool the whole room down, and the electronics at the back get very hot from the effort. The heat generated is greater than the cooling effect of the fridge, meaning the whole room gets hotter!

Quick guys, she's not looking!

WHAT DO ELECTRONS GET UP TO WHEN YOU'RE NOT LOOKING?

About 100 years ago, scientists made a mind-blowing discovery—things we think of as particles (like atoms) can behave like waves, and things we think of as waves (like light) can behave as particles! This seemed so unbelievable that everyone wanted to test it, but, incredibly, these researchers then discovered something even stranger. If somebody was watching the experiment, the electrons behaved differently than when nobody was looking! What on earth was going on? Scientists have spent decades working to try and understand this peculiar behavior.

BREWING THE PERFECT COFFEE

To make a cup of coffee you need boiling water. And water boils at 212°F (100°C), right? Well, it depends where you are. Water boils at 154°F (68°C) at the top of Mount Everest and 356°F (180°C) on Jupiter! This may sound strange, but the temperature something boils at actually depends on the pressure. The pressure at the top of Everest is three times less than at sea level, so water can boil at a much lower temperature. On the other hand, Jupiter has ten times the pressure of Earth, so water boils at a much higher temperature.

MARIE CURIE'S NOTEBOOKS ARE STILL RADIOACTIVE

Marie Curie (1867–1934) was a scientist famous for discovering radioactivity. But did you know that more than 100 years after her death, all of her equipment, including her notebooks, is still radioactive? Radioactive elements release damaging energy and particles as they go through a process called radioactive decay. Unfortunately, Curie didn't know that this radiation was dangerous, and during her 40 years of research her notebooks became covered in these harmful chemicals (Curie herself perished as a result of radioactive poisoning). One of the elements she discovered, radium, stays radioactive for over a thousand years, so the notebooks won't be safe to touch for some time!

THE SALEM WITCH TRIALS WERE PROBABLY CAUSED BY A FUNGUS

In December 1691 chaos struck a Massachusetts village! Girls and young women suddenly started behaving oddly—some slurred their speech, some had fits, and some were manic and hysterical. Doctors couldn't explain this strange behavior and blamed the symptoms on witchcraft! However, there may be a much simpler scientific explanation. The summer of 1691 was warm and wet, which just happens to be the ideal growing conditions for a poisonous grain fungus called ergot. We now know that ergot can cause hallucinations and fits, so it's possible that the "witchcraft" was just down to a bit of moldy bread!

You're a bewitching dancer, Mary.

CHAPTER 8

USELESS EARTH KNOWLEDGE

In which the reader will meet lava that moves as fast as a tiger, debate which of Earth's mountains is the tallest, try to find Australia, and solve the mystery of rocks that move in the night.

WHAT'S AT THE END OF THE RAINBOW?

There is something magical about seeing a bright-colored arch appear over the horizon after a big storm... and that's only half of the picture! From the ground, our eyes can only see the portion of rainbows that appears over the horizon, while the rest is obscured by the landscape. But if you ever are lucky enough to spot one from a very high mountain or, even better, from a plane, you would see that in fact rainbows are perfect rings of color. That does mean you're unlikely to find a pot of gold at the end of the rainbow, though, as they never end!

159

MOST VOLCANOES ON EARTH ARE UNDER THE WAVES

BIRDS COME AND CHECK OUT THE NEW ISLANDS, **POOPING OUT SEEDS** THAT WILL GROW INTO THE ISLANDS'S FIRST PLANTS!

THE **HAWAIIAN ISLANDS** WERE CREATED BY UNDERWATER VOLCANIC ERUPTIONS.

IF YOU PLOT EVERY SINGLE VOLCANO ON EARTH ON A MAP, YOU WOULD BE ABLE TO **TRACE THE SHAPES** OF MANY TECTONIC PLATES BY JUST JOINING THE DOTS!

161

Swim to the bottom of the ocean and you might be surprised by what you find there... Running along the bottom of every single one of the world's oceans is an interconnected chain of volcanoes! Earth's crust is a bit like a jigsaw, made up of large pieces called tectonic plates that rub up against each other. The impressive volcano chains mark the locations of boundaries between pairs of these plates that are moving away from each other. The underwater volcanoes spew up molten lava, which can harden into rock and create new islands!

THE BIGGEST DESERT IN THE WORLD IS COVERED IN ICE

Picture a desert in your head. What do you see? Let me guess... a windswept, sandy landscape with little or no life. However, deserts don't need to have sand in them! Instead, they are defined as areas of the world that receive very little or no precipitation (that means rain, snow, fog, or mist). As a result there are coastal, tropical, and polar deserts! While the coastal parts of Antarctica do get a little rain, there are areas of the continent that have not seen any in over 14 MILLION YEARS! That earns Antarctica the title of the world's biggest desert.

THERE IS ENOUGH GOLD ON EARTH TO COAT THE WHOLE PLANET

Although you would need to dig very, very deep, all the way to the planet's core, to get enough! Unlike the rest of Earth's layers, which are formed by mineral-rich rocks, the core is made up almost entirely of metals, mostly iron and nickel but also some others, including gold. Given the core's HUGE size (about 70 percent of the size of our moon), even though the concentration of gold in it is very low, it would be enough for you to cover the planet in a layer over 20 in (50 cm) thick.

AUSTRALIA IS WIDER THAN THE MOON

When we plot the features of Earth onto a map, they get somewhat distorted because Earth is a sphere, but most maps are flat rectangles. For example, continents located near the equator are made to look smaller than they really are by many maps. One example of a continent that is quite a lot bigger than it usually appears is Australia. Coast to coast, it measures almost 2,500 miles (4,000 km), which is wider than the Moon!

THE EARTH ISN'T FLAT... BUT IT ISN'T PERFECTLY ROUND

If you had a huge measuring tape and used it to measure the distance between the center of the Earth and sea level, you would find that at the equator that distance is greater than at the poles! The Earth is an "oblate spheroid," which is a complicated way of saying it is squished at the top and bottom... and plumper around its waistline! This is because as the Earth spins it generates forces that push it outward around the equator. The same forces make your arms come up if you spin fast on your feet—give it a go!

The very earliest humans appeared on Earth just over 2 million years ago. That might seem like a really long time ago... until you consider the Earth is over 4.5 billion years old. Homo sapiens, the species that you and everyone on the planet today belong to, appeared only around 300,000 years ago, so from the planet's perspective, we are very recent inhabitants. And yet, while to us Earth seems really old, it really isn't either: the universe is over three times older (just under 14 billion years old)!

EARTH IS OVER 20,000 TIMES OLDER THAN HUMANS

EVEREST IS NOT THE WORLD'S TALLEST MOUNTAIN

Or is it? It depends on how you measure a mountain's height. Measuring from its base to the very highest point, the Mauna Kea volcano in Hawaii wins! Or it would, but most of the time mountain heights are measured as the difference between their highest point and sea level—and over half of Mauna Kea is actually underwater! Which would make Everest the tallest. Which do you think is the tallest mountain?

I've climbed the world's tallest mountain!

SO HAVE I!

SAVE THE ICE!

The world is getting warmer because of the actions of humans. Almost all of Earth's land ice is located in ice sheets and glaciers. In total, they account for approximately 12 percent of the planet's surface. The biggest is the Antarctic Ice Sheet, which covers just over 8 percent of Earth. If that alone melted, sea levels would rise by nearly 200 ft (60 m), submerging most coastal areas and affecting billions of people. If all of the land ice in the world melted, the sea level would rise by almost 230 ft (70 m). Visiting cities like Barcelona, London, New York, Shanghai, Tokyo, or Lisbon would require you to wear diving equipment. It just shows—we need to take climate change seriously!

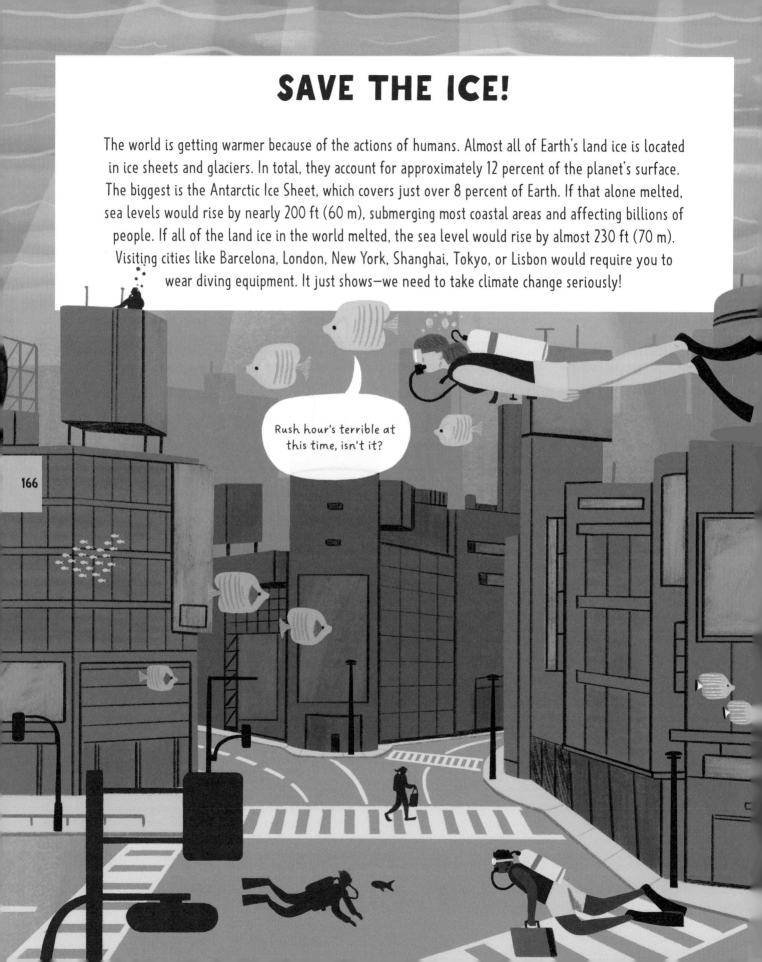

AFRICA X TWO

Along the eastern part of Africa, volcanoes can be seen clustering around large fractures extending hundreds of miles. These tears in the ground are so big that they are visible from space! From up there, Africa looks just like it is breaking into two pieces... and that's exactly what is happening. Over the next few tens of millions of years, the horn of Africa is likely to continue moving east, separating from the rest of the continent, with a new ocean forming between them.

THE INSIDE OF THE EARTH IS GREEN

Did you think it was red and molten? A bit like the lava that comes out of volcanoes? Most people do, but that is far from the truth! The Earth's mantle (the layer between the outer crust and the planet's core) accounts for about 84 percent of the planet, and is largely made up of a type of rock called peridotite. Peridotite contains high amounts of the mineral olivine, and olivine is green—olive green to be precise. So if you brought some mantle rocks up to the surface and let them cool down that is the color you'd see!

IN THE TIME IT TAKES YOU TO READ THIS PAGE, YOU WILL HAVE TRAVELED 1,000 MILES (1,600 KM) THROUGH SPACE

Get you, you little speed demon! It takes Earth 365 days to travel 584 million miles around the Sun. Do the math and you'll find that Earth is traveling at around 67,000 miles (108,000 km) an hour along its orbit. So how come we don't feel like we're moving? The reason is quite simple—we only feel motion when we experience speed changes, like an accelerating car or a bus breaking suddenly, but Earth's speed is constant. Imagine if it wasn't! It probably wouldn't be a very enjoyable ride...

IF EARTH WERE THE SIZE OF AN APPLE, THE CRUST WOULD BE THINNER THAN ITS SKIN

The outermost layer of our planet, where all life as we know it exists, is called the crust. Its thickness varies from place to place, from 3–4 miles (5–7 km) in the oceans to 22–45 miles (35–70 km) in mountainous regions. That means that the crust only makes up about 1 percent of Earth's total thickness, from the surface to the center of the core. And yet, the farthest humans have been able to drill into the crust is only 7 miles (12 km)! One of the reasons why it is hard to dig deeper is that with every mile the temperature increases dramatically, so things get very hot very quickly!

I'm behind you...

IN DEATH VALLEY, HUGE ROCKS MOVE ON THEIR OWN WHEN NOBODY IS LOOKING

Imagine if you were walking on a flat sandy valley, came across a track on the ground and following it led you to a solitary rock. How on Earth can a rock move by itself?

These rocks are known as "sailing stones," and the mystery of their movements was solved thanks to time-lapse photography and GPS technology. It turns out, the valley floors sometimes flood with a very thin layer of water that, in cold winter nights, freezes over. As it melts in the morning, thin floating ice panels pushed by the wind drag the rocks along the sand, before melting away and leaving the mystery behind!

BOO!

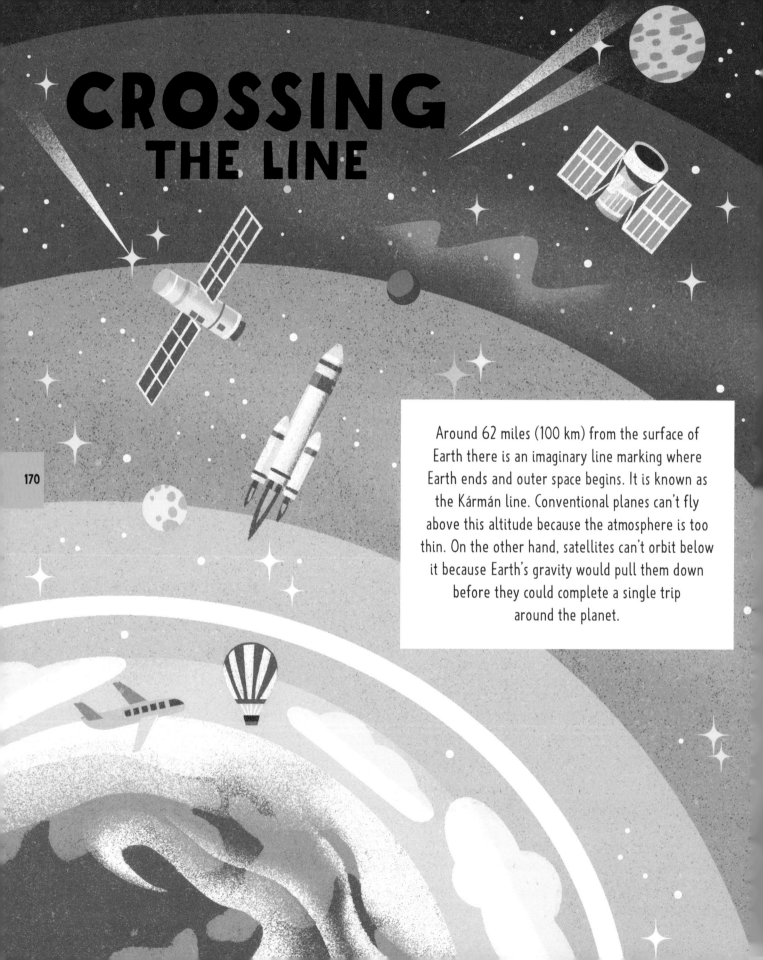

CROSSING
THE LINE

Around 62 miles (100 km) from the surface of Earth there is an imaginary line marking where Earth ends and outer space begins. It is known as the Kármán line. Conventional planes can't fly above this altitude because the atmosphere is too thin. On the other hand, satellites can't orbit below it because Earth's gravity would pull them down before they could complete a single trip around the planet.

GETTING AWAY FROM IT ALL

There are places on Earth known as "poles of inaccessibility"—regions so isolated that they are considered the hardest to reach (or to come back from if you happen to get lost there!). One of them is Point Nemo, in the Pacific Ocean, the most remote location anywhere within the planet's oceans. There is no land within a 1,600-mile (2,575-km) radius of it. If you ever get lost at sea, you will have a better chance to get back to dry land from anywhere but there!

AUSTRALIA IS NOT WHERE YOU THINK IT IS

I'm over here!

Within seconds, our phones can figure out the best way to get us from where we are to where we want to be using satellites. But what happens when the destination is onboard a tectonic plate that is moving so fast that its coordinates change over time? Meet our good friend Australia. Every year, it moves 3 in (8 cm) northeast, so with the passing of time, nothing is where we thought it was!

EARTH'S HISTORY BOOKS ARE WRITTEN ON ROCKS

If you poke your finger into soft sediment, like a sandy beach, it leaves a mark. As that sediment hardens to become a rock, it is possible for such imprints to become fossilized. As a result, those rocks become really useful calendar entries for events in Earth's life! For example, we know when and where certain dinosaurs were walking around by the ages and locations of the rocks they left their footprints on. Or that rain was falling on Earth as early as 2.7 billion years ago, because raindrop marks can be found on rocks that age. Fossils can be found pretty much anywhere, so get out and see what you can find!

THERE ARE **FOSSIL FISH** AT THE TOP OF THE HIMALAYA MOUNTAINS! THAT'S BECAUSE THE ROCKS THAT FORM THEM ONCE LAY AT THE BOTTOM OF AN OCEAN.

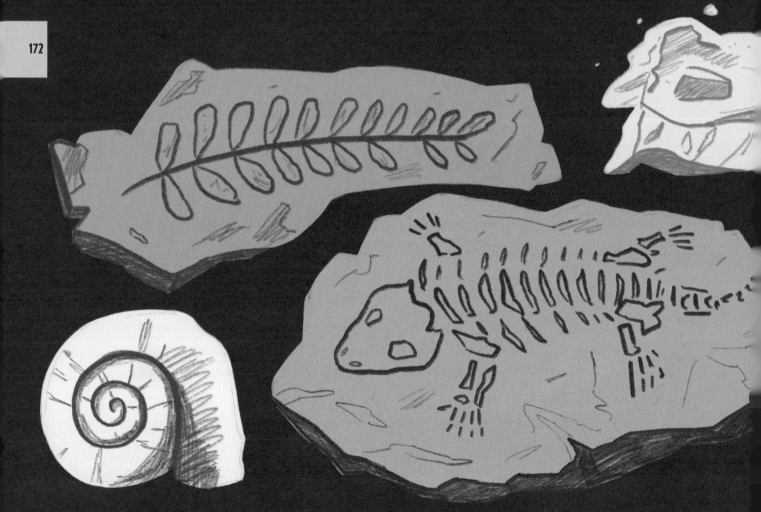

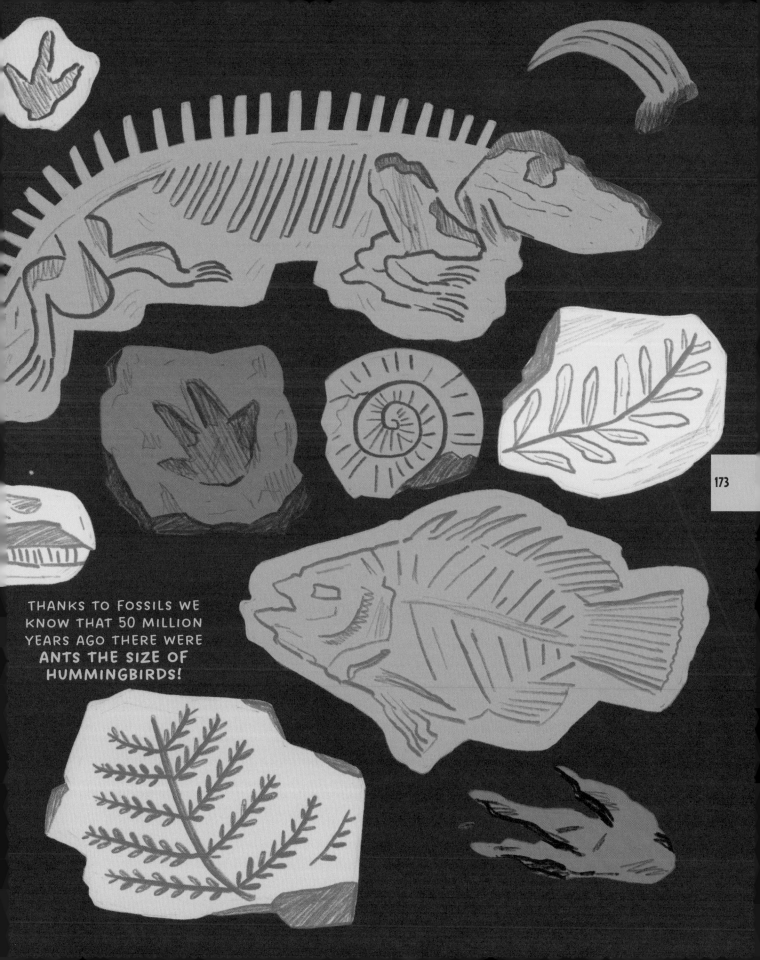

THANKS TO FOSSILS WE
KNOW THAT 50 MILLION
YEARS AGO THERE WERE
**ANTS THE SIZE OF
HUMMINGBIRDS!**

EARTH'S CORE IS AS HOT AS THE SURFACE OF THE SUN

But that doesn't mean there's a star at the center of our planet! At about 10,800°F (6,000°C), the surface of the Sun (and the Earth's core) are relatively mild. At least if you compare their temperature to that of the center of the star, which is estimated to be a whopping 27 million°F (15 million°C). Most of the heat stored inside of the Earth has actually been trapped there for billions of years, ever since the planet's formation. The Earth's outer shell acts a little like a blanket, keeping the heat from escaping into the cold universe.

HOW FAR CAN YOU GO IN A STRAIGHT LINE?

You could sail 20,000 miles (32,000 km) in a straight line, but only walk about 8,000 miles (13,000 km). At least theoretically—nobody has actually done it. The longest straight line you can draw on dry land stretches from Liberia, in West Africa, to the east of China. If you decided to sail instead, you'd be embarking on a journey from Russia to Pakistan, which would not only require you to cross the Pacific Ocean, but also some of the roughest waters on the planet, between South America and Antarctica.

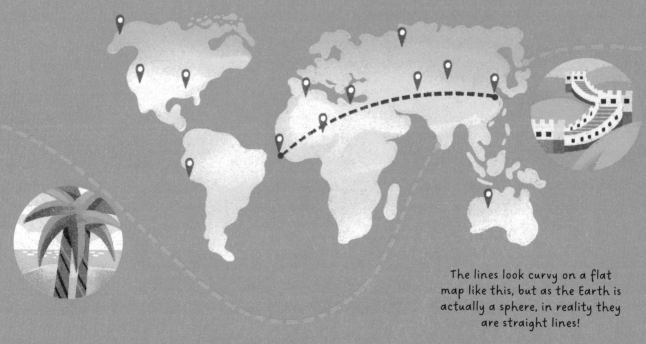

The lines look curvy on a flat map like this, but as the Earth is actually a sphere, in reality they are straight lines!

MOUNT EVEREST FITS INSIDE THE DEEPEST TRENCH IN THE OCEAN

At almost 7 miles (11 km) underwater, Challenger Deep in the Pacific Ocean is Earth's deepest point we know of. So deep in fact that, if you could somehow place Mount Everest at the bottom of it, its peak would still be more than a mile underwater! Challenger Deep is located in the Mariana Trench, a long, curved trough marking the boundary between two oceanic tectonic plates that have been moving toward each other for millions of years.

WE CAN ONLY DRINK LESS THAN 1% OF EARTH'S WATER

Earth is often referred to as "the blue planet," and with good reason—70 percent of it is covered in water (and there is even more under the surface). However, less than 3 percent of all the water on Earth is fresh water and less than half of that is available to us for drinking. The rest is trapped in glaciers, ice caps, and permafrost (a permanently frozen layer of soil, gravel, and sand held together by ice). That is why water is such a precious resource we should look after!

THE LARGEST OCEAN ON EARTH IS GETTING SMALLER EVERY YEAR

Today, the Pacific Ocean covers about a third of Earth's surface, much more than any other water body or land mass. It's so big that, if you look at Earth from a certain angle from space, you can see nothing but water. But if tectonic plates continue moving in the way they move today, 300 million years from now the Pacific will have completely disappeared and a supercontinent will have taken its place. This is because the tectonic plates surrounding this ocean are moving toward each other, riding over the edges of the Pacific plate and making the ocean smaller with every passing day.

LAVA
AS FAST AS A
TIGER

If you spill a liquid on a slope, how fast it flows down depends on the slope's steepness, and what the liquid is. Molasses, for example, would move a lot slower than water. Lava, however, can be frighteningly quick. The fastest ever recorded, at speeds of up to 40 mph (64 kph), occurred during an eruption in 1977 of the Nyiragongo volcano in Africa. That's as fast as a tiger at a sprint, and way faster than the fastest human ever!

177

CHAPTER 9

USELESS
SPACE
KNOWLEDGE

In which the reader will learn how astronauts deal
with poop in space, meet some tortoises who have been
to the Moon, learn how expensive space suits are, and
find out why black holes can turn you into spaghetti.

TRY NOT TO BURP IN SPACE

We're being serious. If you are going to live on the International Space Station, you won't be able to enjoy your favorite sodas. On Earth, thanks to the gravity, when you drink a fizzy drink, the bubbles rise up and separate from any food and liquids. You can then get rid of these gases by burping. In space, however, without the same effects of gravity, the bubbles can't rise and separate. This means you'd burp up a mixture of food, liquids, and gas all at once—very unpleasant!

THE FISH WITH THE GLOWING BONES

If humans are going to live in space one day, floating in space stations or living on Mars where the gravity is weaker than on Earth, we need to understand the effects that this will have on our bones. The Japanese space agency, JAXA, turned to an unusual animal to investigate. Medaka are fish, but not any old fish. They're see-through! This meant the scientists could easily observe their bones and look for changes. Living in a special tank on the International Space Station, the fish were genetically modified so that special bone-building cells would glow under certain lights, allowing scientists to study them in more detail!

THE SHRINKING RED SPOT

Jupiter's Great Red Spot is a huge, violent storm that has been raging on the planet for hundreds of years. It is so big that you could fit the Earth across it, but it used to be bigger... Back in 1979, when the Voyager spacecraft was taking photos of Jupiter, you could fit about three Earths across the storm. What's going on? Well, ahem, we don't actually know. But it looks like the Great Red Spot will soon be the Not-So-Great Red Spot.

CAUSE OF DEATH: SPAGHETTIFICATION

A black hole is an area of such strong gravity that not even light can escape. Black holes come in all sizes, but supermassive black holes are created after a supernova—when a massive star explodes at the end of its life. If you ever got too close to a supermassive black hole, well, let's just say that would be unwise. You would be stretched toward it like a string of spaghetti! In fact, this process is called spaghettification.

FUNNY BUMPING INTO YOU HERE

The Sun and our solar system occupy a tiny corner of space in one of the spiral arms of a galaxy called the Milky Way. This spiral galaxy is a collection of hundreds of thousands of millions of stars, most of which we believe have planet systems around them. The nearest galaxy to us is called the Andromeda galaxy. These next-door neighbors aren't happy with just being near each other, though—they are slowly getting closer! In about 5 billion years they will collide. Eeek!

DON'T WORRY, THIS ISN'T HAPPENING ANY TIME SOON. FIVE BILLION YEARS IS LONGER THAN THE **ENTIRE HISTORY** OF OUR PLANET.

THE MILKY WAY IS MORE THAN **100,000 LIGHT YEARS** WIDE. THAT MEANS IT WOULD TAKE LIGHT (WHICH IS SUPERFAST) 100,000 YEARS TO CROSS IT!

THE UNIVERSE
WAS CREATED
13.8 BILLION YEARS
YEARS AGO IN AN
EXPLOSION CALLED
THE BIG BANG.

AN OUT-OF-THIS-WORLD TOILET

In the micro-gravity of a space station, liquids float around. This means that astronauts have to use a special space toilet to capture all their waste, or there would be poop and pee floating around! The toilet has two compartments. In one, water is removed from solid waste before the poop is burned up in the atmosphere. In the other, pee is collected in a funnel, ready to be cleaned and purified.

THIS ANIMAL CAN SURVIVE IN SPACE

The only animal that has been able to survive in space? That will be the small but mighty tardigrade, also known as a water bear. When conditions get extreme, this microscopic creature goes into a kind of dried-out hibernation state. A 2007 European Space Agency mission called TARDIS (TARDigrades In Space) put the little critters in space for ten days. Despite the cosmic radiation, lack of oxygen, and extreme cold, when returned to Earth they woke up—surprising all of the scientists!

SPACE SUITS ARE REALLY EXPENSIVE

For an astronaut performing a spacewalk, their space suit acts like a personal spaceship. It provides the air they need to breathe, regulates their body temperature, and protects them from the vacuum of space, while allowing them the movement they need to perform their tasks. While some parts of the space suit are ready-made, others such as the gloves are customized for each astronaut. Since the suit is complex and has to work perfectly every time, it comes with a hefty price tag—somewhere in the region of 12 million dollars!

SUNSETS ON MARS ARE BLUE

Mars and Earth have very different atmospheres. Earth's mainly consists of nitrogen and oxygen, while Mars's is mainly carbon dioxide and fine particles of Martian dust. And this difference has a funky impact on sunsets. The light from the Sun is made up of lots of different colors—you can see them all in a rainbow. The particles in the Earth's atmosphere scatter the blue light from the Sun more than other colors. This means the sky looks blue during the day and the sunsets look red. On Mars, however, the atmosphere scatters red light more, so the sky looks redder during the day and sunsets take on a blue tinge!

Do you know any birds that have thought about traveling to space? You might want to put them off the idea. While many animals have successfully been to space, many birds would struggle to eat and drink in a space station. That's because lots of bird species rely on gravity to swallow food and drink. In a microgravity environment, they wouldn't be able to get anything down! That's not to say birds haven't been to space—the Soviet Union sent quails to space, and the USA blasted some chicken eggs out of the atmosphere to conduct experiments on them.

TWEETIE BYE

THE MOON IS EARTH'S BABY

WELL, KIND OF...

Our constant companion in space, the Moon, orbits the Earth once every 28 days. However, the Moon was not always there, and is in fact evidence of an enormous collision in Earth's history! Scientists believe that about 4.5 billion years ago, when the Earth was a very young, hot planet of mostly melted rock and metal, a Mars-sized object collided with it. Material from the Earth and this object was spun out into orbit around the Earth, where it clumped together and eventually formed our Moon.

THIRSTY? FANCY A SWEAT-SHAKE?

In space, water is a valuable resource. It costs a lot of money to send water into space, and so on the International Space Station, as much water as possible must be recycled. Water in the breath, sweat, and even the pee of the astronauts is collected, treated, purified, and recycled by a complicated system called the Water Processing Assembly (WPA). Today around 90 percent of all the waste water on the ISS is recycled into usable drinking water!

THE ULTIMATE SLINGSHOT

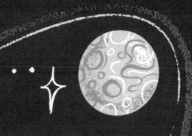

You need a lot of energy to send a spacecraft to the outer planets in our solar system. You could launch all of the fuel you'd need for the journey, but it would be incredibly difficult and expensive. Instead, scientists use gravity and math to perform something called a gravitational slingshot to give the spacecraft a bit of a boost. The spacecraft zips around a planet or moon and takes some energy from it to help it on its way. What a crafty solution!

YOU CAN LOOK INTO THE PAST

Light is the fastest thing in the universe, traveling at a speed of 186,000 miles (300,000 km) per second. But space is big, very big indeed, and the distances that light has to cover to get to us from a star are so huge that it takes time for the light to reach us. Even light from the closest star to us after the Sun, Proxima Centauri, takes more that four years to reach Earth. So when we see the light from stars, we are seeing them as they were hundreds, thousands, or even millions of years ago!

THAT'S MY FAVORITE SUNSET TODAY

Astronauts living on the International Space Station get the most amazing views of the Earth. Sitting in the Cupola, the viewing module of the station, they can see cities lit up at night, spectacular thunderstorms and lightning, and even the northern and southern lights. They orbit the Earth every 90 minutes, which means they also get to experience 16 sunrises and sunsets every day!

SEE YOU LATER!

One of the really useful things left on the Moon by the Apollo astronauts were retroreflectors. These are giant reflectors designed so that scientists can fire lasers at them, which can be bounced back to Earth. By timing how long it takes for light to get to the Moon and come back, scientists can work out how far away the Moon is. And they have discovered that the Moon is moving slowly away at a rate of about 1.5 in (4 cm) a year!

YES, TORTOISES HAVE BEEN TO SPACE

THE TORTOISES **WEREN'T ALLOWED** TO EAT ANYTHING WHILE THEY WERE IN SPACE.

The first animals to go to the Moon and come back were tortoises! Launched by the Soviet Union in 1968 (a year before humans walked on the Moon) the Zond 5 spacecraft carried two Russian steppe tortoises as well as some flies and worms. They flew around the Moon and then returned to Earth safely and in good health. And while they never landed on the surface, they successfully became the first living creatures from Earth to visit another world.

A SQUIRREL MONKEY CALLED **MISS BAKER** WAS SENT TO SPACE BY NASA.

A STRAY DOG FROM MOSCOW CALLED **LAIKA** IS THE MOST FAMOUS SPACE-FARING ANIMAL.

THE EARTH, IT IS A-WOBBLIN'

The pole star, Polaris, has long been used by explorers in Earth's northern hemisphere to navigate. Since the Earth is spinning on its axis, the stars in the night sky appear to move over the course of a night—apart from Polaris. If you imagine that you extended a line through the Earth and its north pole into space, the first star it would point at is Polaris. But the Earth also has a bit of a wobble, and this means that in a few tens of thousands of years, the North Pole will point at a new star, and that star will become our pole star! Luckily today's explorers have satellites to help them navigate...

SUCH A DRAG

The International Space Station orbits the Earth about 250 miles (400 km) above the surface. While this height is well above most of Earth's atmosphere, there is still just enough atmosphere to cause a small amount of drag. This drag is enough to make the ISS lose about 295 ft (90 m) of altitude a day. But never fear, the ISS is up to the challenge. It performs regular boosts where engines are fired to raise its orbit.

FOOTPRINTS ON THE MOON MIGHT BE THERE FOREVER

When Neil Armstrong and Buzz Aldrin first set foot on the Moon in 1969, they knew that they were making history. They were also making footprints. With no atmosphere and no wind, the footprints the Apollo astronauts left on the surface won't ever be blown away! In fact, the only thing that can wear the footprints down is the gradual impact of tiny micrometeorites, and this could take up to 100 million years. These historic footprints can still be seen by passing spacecraft, or indeed you—if you ever make it to the Moon.

SUPER SOLAR POWER

The Sun is a giant nuclear reactor. Every second the Sun squashes together 600 million tons of hydrogen, turning it into helium, which produces an unimaginably large amount of energy. Only a small amount of this energy makes it to us here on Earth, in the form of light and heat. Despite this, more solar energy hits the surface of the Earth every hour than all the people on the planet use in a year!

SPINNING STARS

There are many different types of star in the universe, all at different stages of their life. Neutron stars are one of the strangest. These stars are the collapsed core of a once giant star that reached the end of its life and exploded (this explosion is called a supernova). All stars rotate, but when the core of this star shrinks in size, the rate of rotation increases. That means that these stars spin—fast! In fact, neutron stars have been observed to spin more than 600 times every second. Good thing they don't get dizzy!

EXCUSE ME, ARE YOU LOST?

Not all planets orbit a star. Rogue planets do things their own way, and wander through space alone. Scientists have discovered one particularly giant rogue planet called SIMP J01365663+0933473 (catchy). It is nearly 13 times more massive than Jupiter and has such strong magnetic fields that scientists have been able to detect aurora (northern and southern lights) on it!

THE MOST DANGEROUS MEAL IN HISTORY

When Yuri Gagarin became the first human to go to space, he also became the first person to eat in space. Scientists didn't know for certain whether he'd be able to swallow properly in space, so Yuri had to be very careful. On April 12, 1961, he took a tube of beef and liver paste and carefully squeezed it into his mouth, proving that humans could swallow in space. He celebrated with a dessert of chocolate sauce, also squeezed from a tube.

THE FIRST WOMAN TO GO TO SPACE WAS A RUSSIAN COSMONAUT CALLED **VALENTINA TERESHKOVA.**

TODAY, MOST SPACE FOOD IS **FREEZE-DRIED** TO PRESERVE IT FOR A LONG TIME.

CCCP

199

DESPITE SURVIVING IN SPACE, YURI GAGARIN WAS SADLY **KILLED** WHILE TRAINING FOR A SECOND SPACEFLIGHT.

GLOSSARY

Algae
A plant-like organism that uses sunlight to create energy.

Amphibian
A type of animal that can live in water and on land. Examples include frogs, toads, and salamanders.

Anesthetic
A drug that puts a patient to sleep so they can be operated on by a surgeon.

Archaeologist
Someone who studies the past using the objects people have left behind.

Arthritis
A medical condition that causes pain in the joints.

Artificial intelligence
When computers or machines are able to think for themselves, without human help. Also known as AI.

Astronomer
A scientist who studies space.

Atoms
The tiny particles or building blocks found inside everything—including you!

Bibliosmia
The act of smelling books.

Big Bang
The huge explosion 13.8 billion years ago that created the universe and everything in it.

Bioluminescence
The ability of some animals, such as glowworms and deep-sea fish, to create their own light.

Bullet train
A superfast Japanese train.

Cacao bean
The seed that is the main ingredient in chocolate.

Camouflage
The ability to blend into an environment as a form of disguise.

Carnivore
A meat-eater.

Cartilage
A soft material in your body. Your nose and ears are made of cartilage.

Čimburijada
A scrambled egg festival held every year in Bosnia and Herzegovina.

Climate change
The increasingly rapid change in Earth's long-term weather patterns attributed to humans burning fossil fuels such as oil and coal.

Computer program
A series of instructions that tells a computer what to do.

Coprolite
A fossilized poop.

Core
The center of a planet, moon, or star.

Court minstrel
A type of medieval entertainer, for example a jester.

Ecosystem
Plants and animals that interact with each other and their environment.

Electrons
Electrically charged particles found inside atoms.

Elizabethan England
England during the reign of Queen Elizabeth I (1558–1603).

Equator
An imaginary line around the center of the Earth, dividing it into northern and southern hemispheres.

Exoskeleton
The hard outer casing of some animals, such as insects.

Extinction
When all members of a species die.

Fossil
A prehistoric animal or plant (or even a footprint!) that has turned to rock over millions of years.

Gastric juice
The mix of chemicals in your stomach that help to break down food.

Geothermal vent
A place where heat from inside the Earth rises to the surface, for example a hot spring or a geyser.

Glacier
A slow-moving frozen river.

Gravity
The force that attracts objects to each other. Gravity keeps your feet on the ground!

Homo sapiens
The name of our species of human. You are a Homo sapiens!

Hydrogen
A gas, common across the universe and inside you.

Industrial Revolution
A period of dramatic change in the 18th and 19th centuries, during which parts of the world moved from mostly farming to manufacturing goods in factories.

Intestines
Fleshy tubes responsible for absorbing nutrients from food digested in your stomach. These organs are part of the digestive system.

Invertebrate
An animal without a backbone. Insects, crabs, and spiders are examples of invertebrates.

JAXA
The Japanese space agency.

Jenny Haniver
A dried skate, ray, or fish made to look like a petrified mermaid.

Kármán line
An imaginary line marking where Earth ends and outer space begins.

La Tomatina
A tomato fight held every year in Spain.

Loincloth
An ancient form of clothing comprised of a piece of fabric wrapped around one's waist.

Mammal
A type of animal that is usually furry and feeds its babies with milk. Humans, dogs, and cats are examples of mammals.

Mantle
The layer in a planet between the outer crust and the planet's core.

Megacity
A city with a population of 10 million people or more.

Migration
The seasonal movement of animals to a new place, usually in search of food or somewhere to raise their babies.

NASA
The USA's space agency.

Neanderthal
An extinct species of human with a big brain that lived in Europe and Asia.

Nerve cells
The cells that deliver messages from different parts of your body to your brain, for example if something is causing you pain.

Non-Newtonian fluid
A fluid that behaves like both a fluid and a solid.

Nucleus
The center of an atom, made up of smaller particles called protons and neutrons.

Orbit
The path an object in space takes around a planet, moon, or star. For example, the Earth orbits the Sun.

Organ
A part of the body that has a specific job. For example your heart is an organ that pumps blood around your body.

Oxygen
A gas found in the air, which we need to breathe.

Paleontologist
A scientist who studies fossils and prehistoric life.

Permafrost
A permanently frozen layer of soil, gravel, and sand held together by ice.

Pharaoh
An ancient Egyptian ruler.

Philosopher
Someone who thinks about the meaning of life and existence.

Pilgrimage
A journey to a place considered sacred, often associated with religion.

Polterabend
The German custom of smashing plates, cups, and bowls the night before someone gets married.

Predator
An animal that hunts and eats other animals.

Prey
An animal that is hunted and eaten by other animals.

Pterosaur
A type of prehistoric flying reptile, often confused with dinosaurs. Pterosaur means "winged reptile."

Reptile
A type of animal that lays eggs and has scales. Lizards, crocodiles, and turtles are examples of reptiles.

Saliva
Another word for spit.

Salt flat
Land covered in a crust of salt, which was left behind by evaporated rivers, seas, or lakes.

Satellite
An object that orbits another object in space.

Sauropod
Long-necked dinosaurs that ate plants. Examples include Diplodocus and Brachiosaurus.

Sonar
A way of detecting where objects are underwater by sending out sound waves and waiting for them to bounce back off the objects.

Spanish Armada
A large fleet of Spanish ships sent to conquer England in 1588.

Supernova
An exploding star.

Tardigrade
A microscopic creature that can withstand all sorts of inhospitable conditions.

Tectonic plates
Large slabs of rock that cover the Earth's surface, a bit like jigsaw pieces. Volcanoes and earthquakes occur where tectonic plates meet.

Trace fossil
A fossil made by a mark an animal leaves behind, for example a footprint.

Uncontacted group
A group of people who have had no contact with the outside world, typically tribes in remote parts of the world.

Urolite
A fossil created by pee denting the ground!

US Civil War
An internal war fought in the USA from 1861 to 1865, which resulted in the end of slavery in that country.

Vertebrae
The bones that make up your spine (backbone).

Villi
The fingerlike tendrils that cover the inside of your intestines.

Wilhelm scream
A famous sound effect of a man pretending to be bitten by an alligator, used in many films and video games.

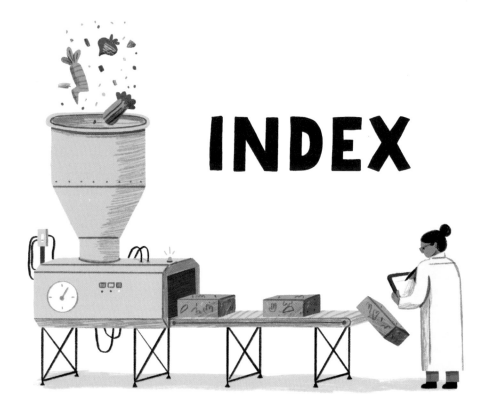

INDEX

205

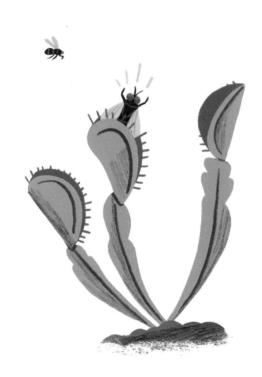

This has been a

NEON SQUID

production

Authors: Dr. Brittney G. Borowiec,
Dr. Victoria Atkinson, Laura Buller,
Dr. Yara Haridy, Anna Goldfield,
Dr. Lucia Perez Diaz, and Sophie Allan

Illustrators: Hannah Li,
Alexander Mostov, and Liz Kay

Editorial Assistant: Malu Rocha
US Editor: Jill Freshney
Proofreader: Joseph Barnes
Indexer: Elizabeth Wise